LIVING OUT THE WHOLE GOSPEL

COMMISSIONED TO LOVE

BY

PASTOR JOHN P. PERKINS
AND ANTHONY D. BOBO, JR.

Handwritten annotations:

To the Great Pastor Brenda, This is... I still Happy New... want my book... hand back.

John 13:35

JPB 1/6/20

Happy New Year

Please look in the Book and find that you are a inspiration

I love you dear! Blessings.

Copyright © 2020 John P. Perkins and Anthony D. Bobo, Jr.

All rights reserved. No part of this publication may be reproduced, stored in a retrieval system, or transmitted, in any form or by any means, electronic, mechanical, photocopying, recording, or otherwise, without the prior written permission of the Publisher.

Citations from the Bible are from the New International Version unless otherwise noted. KJV, The Message, and Living Bible also used.

Cover and Interior Images by Andre Fonseca
Original cover photo by Paul Hanaoka on Unsplash
Layout by Elena Reznikova
Reflection Questions: I AM Intercultural

I AM Intercultural™ is a trademark of Excegent Communication, LLC

Paperback: ISBN-13: 978-1-940105-80-2
Hardcover: ISBN-13: 978-1-940105-81-9
eBook: ISBN-13: 978-1-940105-82-6

Published by I AM Intercultural, an imprint of Excegent Communication, LLC
Watertown, MN

https://www.iamintercultural.com

Find more resources related to this book at https://commissioncircles.com

TABLE OF CONTENTS

FOREWORD
WAYNE "COACH" GORDON

THE CHRISTIAN CHURCH HAS TAKEN a hit in recent years, and for very good reasons in some situations. It is particularly true with younger people who are looking for something more authentic, with integrity that deals honestly with real societal struggles. The Millennials and younger generations are tired of the church saying one thing and doing another. There has been a breach of trust with the community by the church. Many of these breaks involve moral failures or misuse of money by Christian church leaders. But even more so the lack of dealing with Justice concerns that include racism, the industrial prison complex, neglecting the poor, and recently immigration. The church has lagged behind society and has not been leading the way through these problems.

I've had the privilege of knowing John Phillip Perkins most of his life, including officiating at his wedding and serving as an advisor for Common Ground Covenant Church. I have a special and tender love for John, his wife Patrice and their children. I met Anthony D. Bobo, Jr. through John and although I do not know him as intimately, I have found him to also be a man of integrity and deep commitment to Christ. That's why it is so exciting for me to write the forward for this timely book.

As one of the founders of the Christian Community Development Association I truly believe that Christian Community Development is a trusted and proven philosophy of ministry that helps us live out the great commandment in Scripture. Christian Community Development has been an effective tool in transforming communities all throughout the world. I love the way John and Anthony have woven Christian Community Development in practical ways, guiding churches for effective ministry outside the four walls of the local church. John and Anthony bring us back to the church leading in society and demonstrating hands-on ways of **leading** people, **living** among the people, **loving** the people, and **learning** from the people. This concept is very Biblical and Christ-centered. Our younger American culture is waiting for the church to step up and be the church. We as the church are called to love our community and to lead it into the future. I am confident both in the ministry and the writing of John and Anthony to help us do this.

This book by John P. Perkins and Anthony D. Bobo, Jr. is refreshing. Having both grown up in ministry families has given them a good understanding and love of the church yet looking with fresh eyes for practical ways to live out the Kingdom of God, particularly for the younger generation. As young African American leaders they are uniquely qualified to help us see new ways of ministry while applying proven Biblical truths. John and Anthony already are having a positive influence and impact for the Kingdom. For the church to be relevant today it is essential that we must get back to living out the great commandment of loving God and loving our neighbor. As Christians we must be in love with God and love Him with everything we have while at the same time being concerned for other people. Getting involved in the difficult issues of our day, speaking and living out the truths of scripture is critical for the church to reach the younger generation. We are **"Commissioned to love."** Yes, we are to be **"The Hands and Feet of Jesus in a hurting world."**

ACKNOWLEDGEMENTS

JOHN— I want to recognize my bride Patrice and our three children (Sarah, John, and Jonathan) for helping me to show up as the man and the minister God requires of me. Special thanks to Common Ground Church (this is your book too) for supporting every effort in the ministry and living out what is in the following pages!

ANTHONY— I want to recognize my wife Stephanie and our two children (Rebekah and Isaiah) who see me at my best and my worst and love me through it all. A special thanks to The Joseph Factor Group for the excellent spirit, collaboration, and friendship continuing to support work in people's lives, our communities, and ministries throughout this country.

Collectively, we are grateful to our ancestors who continue to inspire us, drive us, and lead us. Their voices, sacrifices, and actions continue to ring in our ears and our hearts today. We can't forget all those that support us, believe in us, and are pushing us as we strive to do the will of God.

PREFACE

THIS BOOK, COMMISSIONED TO LOVE, helps us as Christians, as leaders, and as the Church to engage the whole Gospel. Our goal was not to write your typical book! Instead, this is a book of curriculum designed to speak to the church today. Please engage with reflection questions as you go so that we can all get the most out of the book. Let us know what you think too! Send us a note with your thoughts at **tolove@commissioncircles.com**.

The Great Commission is a call for us to Love. Believers today are dealing with the great issue of living out the whole Gospel. We live the Gospel in part, while Jesus desires us to live the whole Gospel. There are huge issues the Church must address as we strive to live out the whole Gospel.

Think about it! What happens when we:

- do evangelism without discipleship?

- pursue justice without reconciliation?

_____

_____

_____

_____

- engage in activities without relationship?

_____

_____

_____

_____

When we do any of these things we present the gospel only in part. But we are commissioned to love: Not just to do a part, but to live out the whole Gospel. Jesus did not call us to Him without revealing the disciplined life of the walk with God—the whole Gospel. God judges us for our sins and also reconciles us through Christ. Jesus preached, taught, and healed while entering into friendship with His disciples, sinners, and the religious of His day.

What does it mean to you that God both judges our sin and also invites us into reconciled life with him?

_____

_____

_____

_____

_____

_____

_____

This book addresses these difficult questions: What is it to do **justice**? What is it to live in **reconciliation**? What does it look like to **evangelism**? What is the process to do **discipleship**? We look at each of these areas through the lens of Christian Community Development and the clarion declaration through Acts 1:8, "...you shall receive power when the Holy Spirit comes upon you and you shall be my witnesses first in Jerusalem, Judea, Samaria, and carry the Gospel to the ends of the earth;" the Great Commission to love in all the world.

As we are Commissioned to Love with the Gospel of Jesus Christ we can break down and break through the barriers which divide rich and poor, Democrat and Republican, urban and suburban. We learn not to be pitted against one another, but rather learning the greatest force in the world that we have is to Love.

What causes divisions between Christians?

_____

_____

_____

_____

_____

_____

_____

How can love overcome the divisions that we find amongst ourselves and in society?

_____

_____

_____

_____

_____

_____

_____

We are Commissioned to Love! The Holy Spirit gives us this power, as we see in Acts 1:8, which is the focus of this book. Living, moving, breathing in this power of God is to share with humanity and to be the hands and feet of Christ (The Living Savior). Luke 10:27, "Love the Lord your God with all your heart and with all your soul and with all your strength and with all your mind'; and, 'Love your neighbor as yourself." This is the "Commission to Love."

> The Holy Spirit is ready to give you power to live out the whole Gospel. Do you want God to empower you to live for Him?

_____

_____

_____

_____

_____

_____

_____

_____

Why is loving our neighbor an important evidence of
God's work in our lives?

_____

_____

_____

_____

_____

_____

_____

_____

JESUS IS THE WAY

IN THIS BOOK, WE SHARE a lot of thoughts about how we should be living. But before we start sharing ideas and concepts, we want to clearly state that Jesus is the way! There are no methods, processes, or operations that lead to salvation other than believing in Jesus Christ, the Savior of the world. These pages will share our insights, passions, and beliefs, but they mean nothing without the power of Christ behind them. Whether we are ministering to those in the streets or preaching in the church, Jesus is the only way to eternal life. He is Lord!

We share for, in honor of, and because of our belief in Jesus Christ. He told us in John 12:32. "And I, when I am lifted up from the earth, will draw all people to myself."

Jesus, We Lift You Up!

Is Jesus the center of your life?

_____

_____

_____

_____

_____

_____

A NEW AGE OF LEADERSHIP:
LEADING, LIVING, LOVING, AND LEARNING

There is a question being asked all over this country, whether in the classrooms, at kitchen tables on Main Street, in boardrooms of corporate America, or in pulpits of the Church. The discussion is framed as succession planning or transition in leadership, and it simply asks, "Where are the next generation of leaders coming from?"

While we (John and Anthony) represent the next generation, we do not feel that we should be held as the "gold standard" models for the next generation. Instead, our goal is to discuss and share what God has put in our hearts about leadership and especially the need in these days for the church to thoughtfully engage issues such as justice, inequality, and diversity.

We are the children of the promise. We are old enough to lead, yet young enough to learn. We are more the beneficiaries of the greatness of our teachers, yet now we are called to help heal the physical, spiritual, financial, and social ills of our time. We are two young men of God, striving to live out the call of God on our lives; we are upholding the legacies of our family while charting a new course in these last days.

What is the legacy that you are living into?

_____

_____

_____

_____

_____

What do you want to continue from the previous generation?

_____

_____

_____

_____

What do you want to change as you leave a legacy behind you?

_____

_____

_____

_____

_____

LEADERSHIP, THE NEXT GENERATION

We both have observed leaders all our lives. With great leaders in our families, communities, and churches, we could not help but be shaped by their words, wisdom, and actions. Similar to the pull of God that has motivated and moved our forebearers, we are drawn to the crisis of our time and its void in leadership.

The world needs leadership from the next generation. Our generation has not directly suffered the depths of the Great Depression, experienced the collaborative force of a Civil Rights Movement, or the victories of women's rights like leadership of previous generations did. Ours is the generation that has been scarred by the drug epidemic in America. We have devastatingly lost loved ones and friends to AIDS and cancer. Voices are silent in the boardroom, and hands are missing in the marketplace because they are behind prison bars—caught in the prison industrial complex.

A USA Today article from a few years back further describes the next generation from which these leaders will be extracted:

"Although today's young adults have been spared the anxiety produced by the Cold War and conscription, their fears are tied to a parade of events — beginning with 9/11 — whose horror and often sheer randomness have notched new lows on our historical totem pole. To name just a few, they include the ongoing fallout at home of wars in the Middle East, an economic collapse, Hurricane Katrina and, most recently, the shooting in Newtown, Conn..."[1]

Even though this group has been scarred by these events, they have not been excused from responsibilities. The article further shares a description of interviews with young people,

"Uniting these far-flung citizens are sentiments of sadness, empathy and optimism befitting a socially networked generation that often turns to each other to escape the media barrage that accompanies each calamity. Profoundly affected yet not paralyzed by the events of their times, these 13- to 17-year olds almost to a person describe a mission to burnish the nation's image to the luster often described by their parents. We, as a country, can be better, they say. We will be better."

Wow! These comments demonstrate the same positive outlook for the future as past generations in the midst of their struggles. This shows us a generation not too different from the past one, with the potential to raise equally great leaders.

What are some strengths of your generation?

In our time, there is a need for a new, focused leadership—leadership that will not only serve, but be willing to speak to tradition and ask, "Is this really serving the people, or serving our need for tradition?" This is the type of leadership that Jesus Christ showed us in Mark 3, when the Pharisees questioned His healing, eating, and serving. Jesus challenged their thoughts, traditions, and threats in the Spirit of love and care. We must operate in that same Spirit as we serve the people of this planet.

Just because one is questioning and presenting solutions that are different than the status quo, this does not make that person the enemy. Neither does it make someone a saint when they stay within tradition and decide not to "push the envelope." This new age of leadership will know, honor, and respect tradition, yet influence and guide innovative directions. We cannot continue to allow the fallen world alone to be the place where people look for creativity. Church leadership can lead the next mobilization of people in the social, political, and economic spheres.

What are some traditions that you think are really good and worth being honored and respected?

_____

_____

_____

_____

_____

_____

What are some traditions that need to be reconsidered or rejected?

_____

_____

_____

_____

_____

_____

Change for its own sake is a problem, but so is stagnation. As a leader in today's world, how do you know what to change and what to keep?

_____

_____

_____

_____

_____

We believe that our approach to leadership will serve in a new and innovative way, but will be built on the old model in a way that maintains our commitments to the values of Jesus. Jesus gave the Great Commission in Acts 1:8. It says, "But you will receive power when the Holy Spirit comes on you; and you will be my witnesses in Jerusalem, and in all Judea and Samaria, and to the ends of the earth." We want to explore this commission in the context of urban America. We will address several exploratory questions:

- **Who will be touched?**
- **Who will be helped?**
- **What are the modern day "Jerusalem, Judea, and Samaria?"**
- **How can we engage those places for Christ?**

We also believe in the processes and methods of Christian Community Development and have seen this approach change places and lives across the world, especially through our experience engaging this work in Mississippi. We will share about the people there and include their stories. Through this sharing we hope to provide the next generation of leaders with examples, inspiration, and ideas to win the world for Christ.

> What does it mean to maintain your commitment to the values of Jesus as you pursue change?

MEET JOHN AND ANTHONY

JOHN: A CHILD OF THE CHURCH

I, John P. Perkins, am the Lead Pastor of Common Ground Covenant Church, a multi-ethnic missional church in Jackson, MS. My vision for Common Ground was developed while serving as the CEO and Executive Director of the Spencer Perkins Center and of the John and Vera Mae Perkins Foundation. Both of these organizations are Christian non-profits focused on youth and community development in the heart of West Jackson. My heart bleeds for the fathers and families in our West Jackson community. I am committed to meeting the holistic needs of our neighbors in West Jackson, where I live with wife Patrice and three children, John-John, Sarah and Jonathan. My family, who is my "first flock," works together in hopes of undergirding Common Ground's mission of Christian Community Development.

Prior to my time in ministry I served as the Executive Chef and Conference Services Manager for Valley Food Services at Eagle Ridge Conference Center in Raymond, MS. It was there, while feeding people in need, that I felt a new calling. The calling was conveyed through the Gospel of John: the message to "Feed my sheep." Jesus' command to Peter moved me to not only meet people's physical needs, but to meet their spiritual and emotional needs as well.

My heart for community and economic development has led Common Ground in efforts to blend church and community by engaging in partnerships with local businesses, schools, and churches in urban West Jackson. While shepherding the congregation, I recognized that the most strongly felt need for many of my congregants was jobs. This recognition led to the establishment of Common Ground Enterprises which currently has a catering business, lawn care service, and barbershop. My new vision, Common Ground Community Development Corporation, is focused on education, workforce development, and housing. I am committed to continue finding and creating resources, so that Common Ground can continue to take the holistic message of the Gospel to the people of urban West Jackson and the rest of the world. We want to effect change in people's hearts so that they can create communities which reflect the Kingdom of God. As a representative of the next generation of Christian leaders, I am excited to continue this work of Christian Community Development.

> **As you think about John's story, what do you hope to learn from him in this book?**

ANTHONY (I WASN'T READY): THE STRATEGIC PLANNING SESSION FOR COMMON GROUND CHURCH PLANT

April 29, 2013, is a day I (Anthony) will never forget. John decided to put my skills and experiences to the test. I had over 20 years of facilitation and strategic planning under my belt, and we sat down and developed the strategic plan for the Common Ground church plant.

We developed questions ahead of time and I conducted individual interviews with stakeholders of the church plant (members of the community, the church, and well-wishers), all leading to a collective meeting to discuss the future of the church. This project was the first time John and I had worked together on our own and everything was on our shoulders. This was the John's pastoral debut, and this was my business's first time creating a strategic plan for a church plant.

We first worked together when I facilitated the inaugural board meeting for the Spencer Perkins Center in Jackson, MS. My Pop (chair of the board at the time) asked me to come in and aid with running the meeting. That day, I met "my brother from another mother." John and I have been beyond friends ever since.

I am the Founder and Senior Associate of The Joseph Factor Group in Clinton, MD. We are a collection of Christian-centered individuals dedicated to assist communities, ministries, and other organizations in reaching their full potential through the processes of visioning, strategic planning, and implementing leading-edge business practices. The Joseph Factor Group supported me as I worked on several projects at the Center. These projects gave John and me opportunities to sit and envision the future for ministry, community, and family. We would talk about the importance of the church and our desire to see a church in West Jackson that effectively engaged the principles we have seen work in our experiences. Who knew (other than God) that these early conversations were not only about supporting each other? They would lead to John's call as Pastor of a church in West Jackson.

It's Meeting Time

We gathered at the Antioch House (one of the facilities of the Spencer Perkins Center). There were over 50 people assembled, and they were all interested in the church plant. We had rich and provoking conversations. We talked about the number of challenges in the community and the opportunities for the church to serve the community. I have never been in a church meeting that was filled with so much positivity.

Toward the end of the meeting, I looked at all the flip charts we had created, reflected over all the discussion, and looked at the faces of all these people. It was the time for me as the facilitator to wrap up the entire experience and point to the future. In spite of all the positivity the group had shared, I was overcome with hopelessness. I saw the number of challenges that we observed, and I felt this small group could not address all these systemic issues. I heard a small voice, and I shared what I heard with the group:

"Many of us look at all the things we raised and wonder, 'How we can do all of this? How can this group meet the needs of the community? It's too much. We cannot!' But I can, you can, we can, do all things through Christ that strengthens us."

Then I knew I was not only committed to John for a moment, but I was committed to this movement of God that He is doing in West Jackson.

Have you had a moment like Anthony did—where you realized that there is great opportunity but also overwhelming need? How can Christ strengthen you in situations of overwhelming need?

_____

_____

_____

WHERE COMMISSION CIRCLES CAME FROM

One evening during the winter of 2013, after a strategic planning session at the Spencer Perkins Center, we (Anthony and John) began to talk as we had on many other occasions. This time was different. We have a special relationship both personally and professionally. We often share concepts we are dealing with as God has called us to ministry and preaching the Gospel. John had recently been invited to present at a university that he had been building a partnership with for a couple of years. As John prepared his messages, we began conversing over his message, which addressed Jesus' call to the disciples to do His work here on earth. What he shared was so clear, we began to build thoughts around the message and were inspired to demonstrate that great call through the "Commission Circles." It is an outline of how Jesus wants us to minister in our circles of influence and to eventually change the world. This thoughtful approach to engaging culture allows the church to ensure it is operating like Christ. This book is the fulfillment of the work we started that evening—we want to share the idea of the Commission Circles with you so that your church and ministry can fully engage the call of Jesus, who has commissioned us to love God with all that we are, and our neighbor as ourselves.

What are you looking forward to in this book? What do you hope to learn?

_____

_____

_____

_____

Is there anything that you are nervous about as you get into this book?

_____

_____

_____

_____

1   From 9/11 to Newtown, Millennial Generation resilient, Marco della Cava,
USA TODAY, January 29, 2013

INTRODUCING
THE COMMISSION CIRCLES

"But you will receive power when the Holy Spirit
comes on you; and you will be my witnesses in
Jerusalem, and in all Judea and Samaria,
and to the ends of the earth."
ACTS 1:8

ACTS 1:8 IS JESUS' COMMISSION to the Believer. When preaching on this scripture, noted theologian Charles H. Spurgeon said, "These are among the last words of our Lord. We greatly prize the last words of good men. Let us set high store by these later words of our ascending Lord."[2] To the Believer, these words of the Savior before His ascension were not only to the original Church but are also instructive to us today.

Jesus told the disciples He was leaving, but His absence did not leave them without work. He shares with them their responsibility to the Kingdom; "be witnesses unto me both in Jerusalem, and in all Judea, and in Samaria, and unto the uttermost part of the earth" (KJV). Jesus instructs them to share with others what they had seen, heard, and known through their experiences. In order to understand what the disciples heard as Jesus issued this commandment we must consider what Jerusalem, Judea, Samaria, and the earth meant to them.

Why might these last words of Jesus to the disciples be especially important?

_____

_____

_____

_____

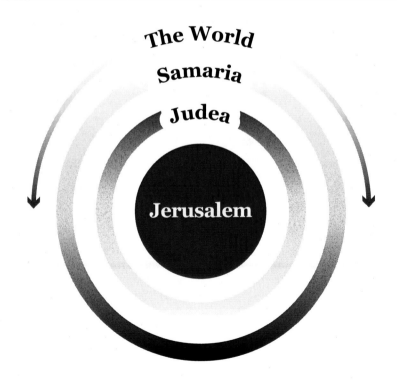

JERUSALEM

To the first-century Jews, Jerusalem represented a special place of God. Biblical scholar P. W. L. Walker notes:

> *The great majority of Jews went up to Jerusalem for the festivals singing the psalms en route; the great majority of Jews heard scripture read regularly in their synagogues. In these ways they acted out, and thereby demonstrated to themselves, their belief that Jerusalem, and its Temple, were the centre of the created order, the place where the creator of the world, who had entered into special covenant with them as a nation, had chosen to place his 'name'.*[3]

When Jesus talked about Jerusalem, He was referring to a place the disciples were very familiar with. A place where they worshiped. A place where they sought the will of God. A place where they saw Jesus work many miracles. It was a place they knew, and Jesus wanted to make sure they continued to represent Him in that city. Jerusalem was the inner circle in their world.

What do you think the disciples had in mind when they heard Jesus calling them to be his disciples in Jerusalem?

_____

_____

_____

THE INNER CIRCLE TODAY

Once, when Pastor John was sharing a message with the staff and students at a Christian university, he outlined how today Jerusalem is the family and the Church. He explained, "The Church is modeled after the family. Home is where the family is nurtured and where people are equipped to do the work of the ministry to affect the world. The family is where love is transferred, and our children are prepared for society." The New Testament authors illustrate this extension of the family of Christ. The author of Hebrews characterizes those who have accepted Christ when he says "Both the one who makes people holy and those who are made holy are of the same family" (Hebrews 2:11). Paul goes further, "God's very own children, adopted into the bosom of his family" (Romans 8:15, Living Bible).

Much like the Jerusalem of yesterday, the family and the Church are in need of the presence of God. Herod built great beautiful buildings in the city of Jerusalem. They were so spectacular that it was said that the area was "a structure more noteworthy than any under the sun."[4] These buildings were built to overwhelm the visitor and to have them think of the greatness of Herod rather than the God of Israel. Today, single parenthood and divorce distract society from God's intention for two parent households and lifelong relationships. The gospel of prosperity, self-worth, and self-determination distracts the Church from God's intention of caring for the poor. Today's Jerusalem needs witnesses of the Risen Savior.

Think about what you wrote above regarding what the disciples had in mind when they heard Jesus calling them to be His witnesses in Jerusalem. What might that mean for you today? How would you describe your "Jerusalem?"

_____

_____

_____

_____

_____

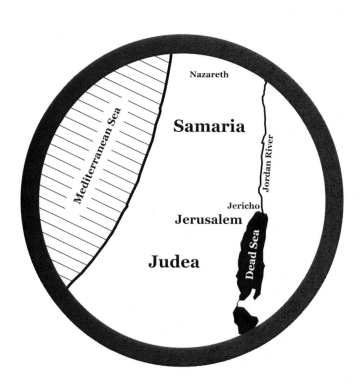

JUDEA

Judea is, geographically, the area surrounding Jerusalem. It too was under the rule of Herod and subject to the Romans. It is remembered in the Scriptures; Jesus was born in Bethlehem of Judea, and later lived in Nazareth in Galilee (Matthew 2:1). Jesus' ministry on earth was largely done throughout Judea, so when the disciples heard Jesus send them to Judea, they reflected on the areas Jesus influenced during His time with them.

The Disciples were with Him when the huge crowds followed Him after witnessing His teaching, preaching, and healing, and they remembered those from Judea who were also witnesses of these actions (Matthew 4:23-25). They remembered how He traveled to the coast in Judea and was confronted by the Pharisees (Matthew 19:1-12). They remembered Judea as the place Jesus worked and saved many. This was the next circle of their lives after Jerusalem.

> What do you think the disciples had in mind when they heard Jesus calling them to be his disciples in Judea?

THE NEXT CIRCLE TODAY

When speaking at a Christian university not long ago, John exhorted his listeners to "be a witness in the area surrounding your home, Impact Your City!" He challenged the group to "take the loving gospel message to the city." We know this message is life changing. Answering the call, we live out God's purpose in the places we work, play, and serve as we respond to Jesus' desire for the modern-day Church to witness in our Judea.

There are several ways that people in ministry feel they can get people to come to Christ. Many feel the media and "high end" marketing is the cause for people coming to Christ. However, studies show even youth ministry should be "high touch." In a 2015 BARNA Group study, the youth surveyed shared about one in four chose the crowd of worshippers (23%). Furthermore, they chose the worshippers because they see Christianity as vibrant and communal.[5] People connect with people. This face-to-face, person-to-person witnessing of the power of Christ in these places of influence fulfills our Lord's desire.

> Think about what you wrote above regarding what the disciples had in mind when they heard Jesus calling them to be His witnesses in Judea. What might that mean for you today? How would you describe your "Judea?"

_____

_____

_____

_____

SAMARIA

Samaria is made up of the "tough places." John explained to the university audience that these are the "front lines and places that make a difference." His foundation for these statements are in John 4:4 where Jesus leaves Judea and was going back to Galilee. The scriptures record "Now he had to go through Samaria."

The Jewish historian Josephus offers a description of the land of Samaria during the time of Christ:

> Now as to the country of Samaria, it lies between Judea and Galilee; it begins at a village that is in the great plain called Ginea, and ends at the Acrabbene toparchy, and is entirely of the same nature with Judea; for both countries are made up of hills and valleys, and are moist enough for agriculture, and are very fruitful. They have abundance of trees, and are full of autumnal fruit, both that which grows wild, and that which is the effect of cultivation. They are not naturally watered by many rivers, but derive their chief moisture from rain-water, of which they have no want; and for those rivers which they have, all their waters are exceeding sweet: by reason also of the excellent grass they have, their cattle yield more milk than do those in other places; and, what is the greatest sign of excellency and of abundance, they each of them are very full of people.[6]

Samaria was clearly the "outer circle" though, because people from Jerusalem would go out of their way to avoid it!

What do you think the disciples had in mind when they heard Jesus calling them to be his disciples in Samaria?

_____

_____

_____

_____

_____

THE OUTER CIRCLE TODAY

While the land in Judea and Samaria might have been very similar, the people were far apart. Not only by miles but by the social culture. Jesus' conversation with a woman of Samaria while He waited by the well underscores this division. John 4:7-9 states,

> When a Samaritan woman came to draw water, Jesus said to her, "Will you give me a drink?" (His disciples had gone into the town to buy food.)

> The Samaritan woman said to him, "You are a Jew and I am a Samaritan woman. How can you ask me for a drink?" (For Jews do not associate with Samaritans.)

The KJV version puts it this way "Jews have no dealings with the Samaritans." Jesus was drawn to go to a place of racial division. What a tough place!?!?

Today we are called to witness in these tough places where racial, social, and class differences have caused a greater distance than the miles between historical Judea and Samaria. Just like Jesus, we need to go there. We go there with the power of faith. We know as John's grandfather Dr. John Perkins outlined "...[T]he implication of making faith practical is that my faith in Christ is relevant to every problem, personal or societal, which I face"[7].

Think about what you wrote above regarding what the disciples had in mind when they heard Jesus calling them to be His witnesses in Samaria. What might that mean for you today? How would you describe your "Samaria?"

Why would Jesus call us to be his witnesses in the places we have prejudices against?

Why might we need to live in the power of the Spirit as we witness in our "Samaria?"

_____

_____

_____

_____

_____

THE ENDS OF THE EARTH
(THE COMPLETED CIRCLE)

Many argue that there are so many issues in the United States that there is no need for international missions. However, the commission of Jesus is also to the "ends of the earth" so we cannot forget South Africa, just like we cannot forget Southeast Washington, DC. We can't forget those who are rebuilding in Haiti from an earthquake just like we cannot forget those who are recovering from floods in Houston. Making sure a girl is able to go to school in Afghanistan is just as important as making sure a girl can go to school in the inner city of Atlanta.

The key is to answer the call of Jesus and live out these Commission Circles. Each outer circle encompasses the inner circle; therefore, this causes the church to daily meet Jesus' commandment. When we live out the Circles, we live out the call of Christ throughout the world. But how do we do this? The Key Components of Christian Community Development, which we discuss in the next chapter, gives us the framework for success.

> What do you think the disciples had in mind when they heard Jesus calling them to be his disciples to the ends of the earth?

_____

_____

_____

_____

_____

> Think about what you wrote above regarding what the disciples had in mind when they heard Jesus calling them to be His witnesses to the ends of the earth. What might that mean for you today?

_____

_____

_____

_____

_____

Why would Jesus call his disciples to be witnesses in each of these different circles?

_____

_____

_____

_____

Which circle is the easiest for you to care about?

_____

_____

_____

Which circle is the easiest for your church to care about?

_____

_____

_____

Which circle is the hardest for you to care about?

_____

_____

_____

Which circle is the hardest for your church to care about?

_____

_____

_____

INTRODUCING THE COMMISSION CIRCLES

In review, describe what you think of when you think of each of the following: your Jerusalem, Judea, Samaria, and the ends of the earth?

_____

_____

_____

_____

_____

Do these circles encompass all ministry here on earth? Is anything missing, and if so why is that missing factor important?

_____

_____

_____

_____

_____

Why are leaders important in each of the Commission Circles?

_____

_____

_____

_____

_____

_____

2   "Witnessing Better Than Knowing the Future;" A Sermon (No. 2330) Intended for Reading on Lord's-Day; October 15th, 1893; Delivered By C. H. SPURGEON; At the Metropolitan Tabernacle, Newington, UK on Thursday Evening, August 29th, 1889.

3   P. W. L. Walker, Jerusalem Past and Present in the Purposes of God, pp. 53 (2nd edn. 1994.) Carlisle: Paternoster. Grand Rapids: Baker.

4   Bible Tutor; 1995 Luther Seminary; 2011 Select Learning; www.bibletutor.com/level1/program/start/places/judea.htm.

5   BARNA Group. "What Millennials Want When They Visit Church." Millennials & Generations. March 4, 2015. https://www.barna.com/research/what-millennials-want-when-they-visit-church/.

6   Josephus (37- after 93 CE), The Jewish War, Book3: CHAPTER 3. Fordham University Jesuit University of New York, http://www.fordham.edu/halsall/ancient/josephus-wara.asp.

7   John M. Perkins; Beyond Charity, The Call To Christian Community Development; Baker Book; 1993; page 140.

CHRISTIAN COMMUNITY DEVELOPMENT

ONE MORNING, MY (JOHN) STAFF asked me to attend the after-school program as part of the ministry at the Spencer Perkins Center. Now, they knew that I usually stayed away from the after-school program. I love the kids, I enjoy being with them, but I know my call is to work with the parents and adults. Frankly, the kids intimidate me. Well this day they convinced me to go.

I arrived at the school and went to the classroom. Because I was new to the setting, the children were attracted to my presence and ran up to me wanting to share with me their writings in their journals. The first journal I read was by a child who wrote, "If I could go anywhere in the world, I would go to New York City because it is a city with bright lights and they call it 'The Big Apple.' And I can only see it on T.V." He was my inspiration to start taking our after-school program students on trips across the country. I talked to the young man's mother. She was the first person

I shared the idea with. When I saw her come into the program, she wouldn't just grab her children and leave as the other mothers did, she would stay and help with homework of her children and the others before leaving.

When I shared my vision of the trip with Ms. Mary, another neighbor at the program, she lit up and she became a supporter of all the trips we did with the kids. Little did I know how Ms. Mary would end up shaping my ministry. Unfortunately, Ms. Mary had some issues with her living conditions. Once we heard about her situation, we offered her the opportunity to be a part of our center's Zechariah 8 Housing Program. This program is based on God's word in Zechariah 8:4-5:

Once again men and women of ripe old age will sit in the streets of Jerusalem, each of them with cane in hand because of their age. The city streets will be filled with boys and girls playing there.

This program takes restored and refurbished houses and makes them affordable homes for those in need. Ms. Mary became a resident and raised her family in one of the homes.

Fast forward to the early days of Common Ground, when it was just in the early stages of being a church plant. We gathered to discuss what this church would be, what would it be like, and who it would attract. I remember like it was yesterday, Ms. Mary stood with tears in her eyes and with trembling voice said, "I want the type of church that will not look at me as a single mother. I don't want to be looked at from my mistakes." Her experience was that churches saw her as immoral and less-than honorable.

Ministering to the heartfelt needs of the people is not a one-way street. It is ministry at its best, even shaping the minds of the "churched" to be open to those who God has called to fellowship. My work with Ms. Mary's son caused me to know her. Ms. Mary's expression and response in that meeting caused our church to know the will of God.

Why are small acts of faithfulness to God important in our lives?

_____

_____

_____

_____

_____

What might John have missed if he hadn't disciplined himself to be present in the community and to listen to its members?

_____

_____

_____

_____

_____

How did Ms. Mary want the church to see her? How do you want the church to see you? How would your church view Ms. Mary? Is that a God view?

_____

_____

_____

_____

_____

_____

8 KEY COMPONENTS OF CHRISTIAN COMMUNITY DEVELOPMENT AND THE COMMISSION CIRCLES

The church is needed in the tough places—the places where the struggles are seen in every facet of life—so that the Kingdom can be realized here on earth (Matthew 6:10). This responsibility is one that should not be taken lightly; it is the call of the believer! In this chapter, we present Christian Community Development as a method of commitment for effective change. The Eight Key Components of Christian Community Development provide a guide for Christian leaders to take their God-given talents and manifest them in real life to generate real impact in the community.

What would it look like for God's kingdom to come and for His will to be done on earth as it is in heaven?

_____

_____

_____

_____

_____

CHRISTIAN COMMUNITY DEVELOPMENT

The founders of the Christianity Community Development Association (CCDA) are John's grandparents, Dr. John M. Perkins and his wife Vera Mae Perkins. Dr. and Mrs. Perkins have dedicated their lives to reconciliation and Christian Community Development. They are not only proclaimers of these philosophies but are also practitioners. In the 1960s, they followed the Lord in relocating their family from California to the struggling community of Mendenhall, Mississippi, to work with the people there. CCDA describes their work,

> *The Perkins' devoted thirty-five years to living out the principles of Christian Community Development in Mississippi and California, leaving behind ministries and churches that are now headed by indigenous Christian leaders.*[8]

The Eight Key Components of Christian Community Development are an outgrowth of Dr. Perkins' three initial principles for community development in poor places. He has traveled internationally discussing "The Three Rs"- relocation, reconciliation, and redistribution. These revolutionary principles have proven to lift communities all over the world.

The expansion of the "Three Rs" has grown into the "Eight Key Components of Christian Community Development," building on the proven success of these elements. The other components were later added by Christians like Wayne Gordon, Mary Nelson, and H. Spees (just to name a few) as they discovered new ways to rebuild poor neighborhoods. History shows that God seems to honor the sacrifices made by His people and creates what only His power can. The Christian Community Development Association website further explains its genesis:

> In 1989, Dr. Perkins called together a group of Christian leaders from across America who were bonded by one significant commitment, expressing the love of Jesus in America's poor communities. Not at arm's length, but at the grassroots level.[9]

Building communities through the power of God is a great calling requiring great commitment. We have captured the call in the first chapter on the Commission Circles and feel that the commitment is demonstrated in the Eight Key Components of Christian Community Development. The philosophy of Christian Community Development (CCD) has been emerging over the last forty years in order to engage and reverse the harsh conditions in poor and suffering areas in the name of Jesus. As Christians, we must be willing to live out what we talk about. In the following pages, we will explore how the Commission Circles are lived out through the Eight Key Components of Christian Community Development.

As a quick refresher, what were the four levels of the commission circles from chapter 1?

_____

_____

_____

_____

Dr. and Mrs. Perkins started on their journey of Christian Community Development in the 1960s, but the Christian Community Development Association wasn't founded until 1989. What might this tell you about the persistence and perseverance required in this kind of work?

_____

_____

_____

_____

_____

The eight principles were developed by multiple leaders from across the country as they added to the work of Dr. and Mrs. Perkins—why is it important to learn from and work with other believers as we engage harsh settings of human suffering?

_____

_____

_____

_____

_____

CCD #1: RELOCATION

When reflecting on Christ's call to "be a witness," Dr. Martin Luther King, Jr. in his sermon "Propagandizing Christianity," preaches the importance of the Christian to share the word of God:

> *He is saying in effect, propagandize my word, spread it, disseminate it, push it into every nook and crook of the universe, carry it to every place and every race, every nation and every village. Propagandize my word to the uttermost part of the earth. This command comes to every generation of Christians. Jesus is still saying to Christians everywhere, ye shall be my witnesses, ye shall be my propaganda agents, ye shall be the spreader of my truth in all the world.*[10]

While some would be concerned with King's use of the word "propagandize," the first component of Development suggest the Christian not only *call out* the words of Christ but *live out* the words of Christ among the hurting and poor.

> King suggests that Jesus wants Christians to be his agents of truth in every corner of the world. This implies *movement*. How might Jesus be calling you to move to make his truth known?

_____

_____

_____

_____

_____

Relocation refers to living the gospel and "desiring for one's neighbor and neighbor's family that which one desires for one's self and family."[11] This is what Jesus expressed to the lawyer when the lawyer asked about the greatest commandment (Matthew 22:35-40). The greatest commandment means to love God with all you are and to "love your neighbor as yourself." By living in these tough places, we grow, not just the people in the community. We care about the churches in the community because we worship there with our neighbors. We care about the pollution in the community because our children could develop asthma along with our neighbor's kids. We care about the lack of recreational centers and parks in the neighborhood because our children do not have a place to play. When we live among the poor and hurting, it is not about "them", it is about the collective "us."

> How does moving into a neighborhood help you not only to be an agent of truth, but also to identify with the lived experience of the people in the neighborhood?

_____

_____

_____

_____

_____

_____

The Commission Circles help us live out (or to witness/propagandize) the Gospel in every space and place by paying attention to the different areas of need in the world. Relocating challenges us. We have ministered from afar—from our places of comfort. To live out the Commission Circles, we cannot abandon the tough places. We must be active in these places. And the best way to do that is to live in them. Most importantly, we must live out the Gospel in them in order to bring people to the loving God, who has made us better.

Jesus might be calling you to consider relocating into a community of need—whether in Jerusalem, Judea, Samaria, or the ends of the earth. This can also include returning to a place you came from or remaining in a difficult location. What does relocation look like in your life?

_____

_____

_____

_____

CCD #2: RECONCILIATION

Reconciliation is paying a price to bring back a relationship. As servants of Christ, we know lives are bettered when someone has relationship with God. And through Christ, God is reconciling man into right relationship with Him (2 Corinthians 5:19). For conditions to change, we have to accept the love Jesus Christ has for us.

What is your story of reconciliation with God?

_____

_____

_____

Looking at the church today, it appears that many of us feel comfortable with bringing people to Christ and then sending them on their way, but this work is just the beginning. There is a price to restore relationships among individuals, races, and cultures. Man and the fall—the introduction of sin into the world—have caused these artificial boundaries for power, position, and money, but these walls must be torn down for us to be reconciled with one another.

> **Where do you see broken relationships in the world today?**

_____

_____

_____

_____

Boesak and Deyoung use the early Church to help us understand how this reconciliation looks:

> These [first century] congregations were a mix of colonized persons and colonizers (or beneficiaries of colonization). When Jews saw Roman soldiers and citizens in their midst, they remembered their oppression. When Jews sat next to Gentiles who benefited from Roman rule, they were painfully aware of their low social status. Every time these assemblies spoke of Jesus crucified, they were reminded of the

Roman state-sponsored terrorism used to kill Jesus and to intimidate Jewish people. Given the brutality and bigotry experienced by Jews as subjects of the Roman Empire, it is difficult to believe that Romans (and others benefiting from their position in the empire) would be invited into Jewish faith communities. But this is what happened.[12]

In America, Church that looks like this would be made up of all people worshipping God together. Not a "black church," a "white church," a "Hispanic church," an "Asian church," a "Native church," all separated, but **God's Church** calling us all into relationship with God while loving, sharing, and serving with God's creation. All races serving on all levels. All races reflected in worship. All races recognized in praise. God's Church reconciling people to one another.

The first century church, as described by Boesak, contained people from all different groups even though the people would have been aware of disparities and wrongs between the groups. What would that look like in today's context?

We want to clearly exclaim, while racial reconciliation is important and is a command to the Church (2 Corinthians 5:18), reconciliation also has to happen in other parts of our society! Boesak and DeYoung offer further insights:

> *Reconciliation is always about more than race. Congregations that become successfully multicultural and multiracial are not fully reconciled unless they are addressing other places of alienation, marginalization, and injustice. Congregations can be racially reconciled but not fully reconciled if they do not include and empower other marginalized persons in their life and leadership as a congregation.*[13]

What do you think are some of the most difficult issues that remain unreconciled in the church today?

Jesus desires for us to work out these "Samaria" issues. These racial, not to mention social and economic, issues are not easy. There are some who believe like the lady at the well, who told Jesus, "Jews don't deal with Samaritans" (John 4:9). Today they will say things like, "Whites will never move to Black communities." Or,

"White people will never submit themselves to Black leadership in Church." These are issues to be addressed with the understanding that this mindset is not of God. For some, this seems undoable. But when it is modeled, that within itself is a "witness" that Jesus tears down the dividing line between race, culture, and class. His love breaks down every wall of division, striving, and separation. Ephesians 2:11–14 says:

> *Therefore, remember that formerly you who are Gentiles by birth and called "uncircumcised" by those who call themselves "the circumcision" (which is done in the body by human hands)— remember that at that time you were separate from Christ, excluded from citizenship in Israel and foreigners to the covenants of the promise, without hope and without God in the world. But now in Christ Jesus you who once were far away have been brought near by the blood of Christ. For he himself is our peace, who has made the two groups one and has destroyed the barrier, the dividing wall of hostility.*

The concept is continued in Verse 19, which says, "For He Himself is our peace, who has made both one, and has broken down the middle wall of separation.... Now, therefore, you are no longer strangers and foreigners, but fellow citizens with the saints and members of the household of God." What's more—the Commission Circles call us to think about reconciliation at every level of our Kingdom responsibility—in our Jerusalem, Judea, Samaria, and the ends of the earth.

Is it easier to trust Jesus for reconciliation between fallen humanity and God, or for reconciliation between human groups that are at odds with each other? What would it look like (practically) if we trust Him for both?

_____

_____

_____

_____

_____

What work is required on our part in order to bring about reconciliation?

_____

_____

_____

_____

_____

CCD #3 REDISTRIBUTION

The 2012 United States presidential campaign was filled with the term "redistribution." Unfortunately, the term became synonymous with socialism and "anti-Americanism." We hope to discuss this concept without the political baggage of 2012 but had to acknowledge the risk before getting into it.

The Christian Community Development Association describes redistribution differently from that politically charged version: "When men and women in the body of Christ are visibly present and living among the poor (relocation), and when people are intentionally loving their neighbor and their neighbor's family the way a person loves him or herself and family (reconciliation), **the result is redistribution, or a just distribution of resources.**"[14] Wow, living and loving among the hurting naturally causes one to redistribute their resources.

Why is it important for followers of Jesus to demonstrate something beyond social/political ideas of what redistribution means?

In what ways is Jesus-centered redistribution costly?

_____

_____

_____

_____

Let's look at redistribution beyond money. The idea of sharing one's influence is another form of redistribution. Most people get their first job through their network—because of someone who knew someone else. Most of us were not polished enough coming out of school to walk into an office and start to work, but we were given a chance. This chance is often from the neighbor suggesting to her office partners that they give the kid an opportunity to work in the mailroom. She redistributed her influence to give that kid a chance.

In what ways has access (including lack of access) to social networks been important to your job history? What about in other areas of life?

_____

_____

_____

_____

Multiply this many times over, and apply it to the human needs, like housing, education, and health. But this is not a one-sided venture; redistributing helps the giver and receiver. We will discuss this further in "Listening to the Community," but let's establish here that the willingness to distribute resources takes listening to one another.

Serving in the Church, community, and tough places takes resources, and we have to be willing to give our all to be a witness. We will have to move beyond the model of giving ten percent of earning (tithe). Redistribution is not only economic; it includes the social, educational, and relational resources that create equal access and opportunity for all humanity.[15] Jesus demands us to witness in all the world. This assures that those places, where we are called, will benefit from our presence in a meaningful manner. As we think about the levels of the Commission Circles, again we are reminded to think about what redistribution might look like in every different layer of our Kingdom responsibility.

While the tithe can be an important discipline, why is this financially focused form of redistribution too narrowly focused? What does it mean to steward all of the resources in your life as a participant in God's kingdom?

_____

_____

_____

_____

CCD #4: LEADERSHIP DEVELOPMENT

To grow leaders within a community is to establish a stabilizing force that can "fill the vacuum of moral, spiritual, and economic leadership that is so prevalent in poor communities."[16] Mere training is not enough; development is accomplished through meaningful relationships. It is similar to the mantra developed by the National Center for Fathering requiring fathers (fathers being the first exposure to God-ordained leadership that both of us experienced) to love, coach, and model for their children.[17] This is the hard work of building through caring, encouraging, and living.

> Have you seen effective leadership provide a stabilizing influence that allows an organization or community to flourish? On the other hand, have you seen absent or poor leadership lead to negative outcomes in a community?

In Christian Community Development, we believe our work "is most effectively done by raising up Christian leaders from the community of need who will remain in the community to live and lead."[18] The goal of developing leaders is to continue to better the community, not to rise up and move out.

This form of leadership development, to stay and serve, is seen throughout the Bible. Moses and Joshua shared this special relationship of leadership development. Joshua observed the actions and was influenced by the leadership of Moses. The scripture describes Joshua as the "servant of Moses."[19] Joshua did not get this loving, coaching, and modeling from Moses to lead other people, but God selected Joshua to lead the people of Israel into the "Promised Land." In fact, God gives Joshua words of encouragement by reflecting on the relationship that Moses and God had, "As I was with Moses, so shall I be with thee."[20] Joshua, who was an indigenous leader among his people, was reassured of his mission to stick with the people of Israel though the memory of his predecessor.

> What do you have to believe is true of the people from a community if you are going to raise up leaders from within that community? What beliefs might keep us from being able to effectively raise up and follow the leadership of people within a community of need?

Developing Christian leaders changes the world and answers Jesus' call to be a "witness throughout all the earth." Dr. Perkins and Pastor Wayne Gordon push leaders beyond the walls of the church into the public square:

> *In developing leaders, the ultimate goal is not to build the Church, but to make disciples and shape our world in the name of Jesus Christ. Yes, we need pastors and deacons and choir directors, but we also need school teachers and businesspeople and athletes and carpenters and nurses and many others to stand for Christian values in their places of employment and in the square.*[21]

The vision is a world transformed by the leadership of insiders with the love of Christ. It is not limited to witnessing in the pulpit on Sunday mornings, but encompasses our lives in the community every day. Imagine what a difference could be made by intentional leadership development in every one of the Commission Circles!

> **Can you think of an example of a leader that has been raised up from within a community and has gone on to make a positive impact on that community and/or in other layers of the Commission Circles?**

54

CCD #5: EMPOWERMENT

Mary Nelson simply says, "empowering is all about power." Nelson further explains that empowerment:

focuses on a transfer of power; and the concept is usually framed within the struggle for power. We in the church shy away from issues of power and transfer of power because we equate it with confrontation and friction. Think of words that come to mind when you mention power. They are probably words about control and domination; thinking that limits our ability to deal with the positive aspects of power. [22]

One cannot effectively develop communities without this positive transfer of power. The Church has moved away from empowerment, but this must be restored. Going beyond the willingness to only interact with those who look, believe, and worship like us is living out what Jesus demonstrated to us. The reason Jesus got into trouble with the established order was His willingness to live with, talk to, and serve those who were different from Him. He shifted the scales and empowered sinners to become believers, whether the woman at the well with human dignity, the publican (tax-collector) with the chance to repay more than he stole, or the thief on the Cross who received eternal life after acknowledging Truth. Jesus empowered through restoring.

When you think of power, do you think of positive or negative things?

_____

_____

_____

_____

What would healthy exercise of power look like in your church? In your community?

_____

_____

_____

_____

Peter and John give us an example of empowerment as they fulfilled Jesus' command to witness. The blind beggar at the gate of the temple pleading for money was willing to listen to the Apostles. Peter told him, "Silver or gold I do not have, but what I do have I give you. In the name of Jesus Christ of Nazareth, walk" (Acts 3:6). Peter heals him, extends his hand to him, and helps the man up. We see the picture of Peter giving him a hand up, but we also see that the man was willing to take the hand and engage in the process.

Many churches give, but they do not empower. If Peter and John had only put a few coins in the blind man's cup, they still would have left him blind and begging. The food pantries, clothing donations, and soup kitchens often leave those that we are trying to help in the same condition. Many times these handouts make us, the helpers, feel good because we can say that we have served hundreds, but is that a hand up or a hand out? Sometimes we proudly say, "We have been giving to this family for generations." Is that empowering or is that enabling?

> Do you think it is more difficult to empower than it is to "just give"? What might keep people giving to others instead of empowering them?

Robert D. Lupton cautions against skipping over the Great Commandment (The Commitment) on the way to fulfilling the Great Commission (The Call).[23] Empowerment in Christian Community Development is what Peter and John showed us as we look into the true needs of those we serve. Yes, feed, but can we also provide opportunities for those who are fed to give back through volunteering? Yes, clothe, but maybe instead of just a clothing donation, we could set up a thrift store employing those in need as well as selling used items at suitable prices. Dr. Martin Luther King said, "True compassion is more than flinging a coin to a beggar; it comes to see that an edifice which produces beggars needs restructuring."[24] Restructure the system through empowering the least, left out, and overlooked. Truthfully, there is no level of the Commission Circles in which empowerment is not needed! Close to home and far away, with those similar and those who are very different, it is necessary for us to empower those we serve.

Think of an issue where people are disadvantaged by the systems that they live in. Describe it:

_____

_____

_____

_____

What would be a practical way to empower those people to live differently?

_____

_____

_____

_____

Why can empowering people help them to understand their humanity better?

_____

_____

_____

_____

_____

CCD #6: WHOLISTIC APPROACH

Dr. Perkins said "It is time for the church, yes, the whole church, to take a whole gospel on a whole mission to the whole world."[25] This statement captures one's attention because this one sentence presents a simple concept difficult for many churches to realize. It is difficult to realize because the problems and issues of justice can only be addressed through the strength of the whole church, the whole gospel, the whole mission. Let's explore.

This idea of the **whole Church** is bigger than the idea of the denomination. It is working as the entire body of Christ. One body that does not segment itself by race, class, or nationality, but is living out the life of Christ within and without the doors of the church. This is the image of the New Testament Church, when it is described in Acts 2:46-47 "Every day they continued to meet together in the temple courts. They broke bread in their homes and ate together with glad and sincere hearts, praising God and enjoying the favor of all the people. And the Lord added to their number daily those who were being saved." This passage models the fellowship of believers, who are living and acting out the common bond of the Lord and Savior Jesus Christ.

What threats do you see to experiencing life as the whole church?

_____

_____

_____

_____

_____

Have you ever experienced anything that reminded you of the whole church? What was it like?

_____

_____

_____

_____

_____

The **whole gospel**. Paul told the Church at Corinth, in 2 Corinthians 5:19, "that God was reconciling the world to himself in Christ, not counting people's sins against them. And he has committed to us the message of reconciliation." The sharing of the good news of the Savior. A Savior who suffered, but His suffering was not for self-aggrandizement or so He would go down into history as a martyr. Rather, He died so we could get back into right relationship with God. Like the prodigal son who is restored from shame to honor, and like the demoniac who is freed from the power of spiritual bondage, we find that there is no part of our life that is not redeemed by Jesus. This is the whole gospel.

> The gospel speaks to every part of a person's life, and to every part of a community's life, but sometimes we have shortchanged the gospel by acting like it is only powerful in a tiny part of our lives. Have you found Jesus to be relevant in every area of your life? What would hold you back from meeting him in every part of your life or every part of your community's life?

Eldin Villanane challenges the status quo in fulfilling the **whole mission** of the Church, "…we must do away with those false dichotomies that would limit the Word of God and define the gospel as either evangelism or social justice."[26] We are not only to bring people to relationship with Christ, but we must also address the social ills of our times. Villanane further explains the whole mission through the whole gospel: "God is concerned for the whole person. Ours is a holistic gospel, responding to the whole needs of the person. …that God has a passionate concern for justice for all—especially the poor, the weak, and the oppressed members of society. God demands justice in the nation."[27] Fulfilling the whole mission guides us to invite people to come into loving relationships with a Savior who commands us to witness for Him in every place. Like Him, we will not keep silent before unjust activities in the church, the streets, or in the marketplace.

> The whole mission involves making the will of God, and the character of God known on earth. How have you seen this done well? What role do you have to play in making God known in fullness—both through evangelism *and* justice?

_____

_____

_____

_____

_____

The **whole world** must be witnessed to. Because of the Commission Circles, what we are presenting does not only mean every place on the globe, but also every place in society. Isaiah captures this when He relates God's word to His people in Isaiah 40:1-5:

"Comfort, comfort my people,"
says your God.
"Speak tenderly to Jerusalem,
and proclaim to her
that her hard service has been completed,
that her sin has been paid for,
that she has received from the Lord's hand
double for all her sins."

A voice of one calling:
"In the wilderness prepare
the way for the Lord;
make straight in the desert
a highway for our God.
Every valley shall be raised up,
every mountain and hill made low;
the rough ground shall become level,
the rugged places a plain.
And the glory of the Lord will be revealed,
and all people will see it together.
For the mouth of the Lord has spoken."

God will use His witnesses to live out His presence in the earth. He will bring justice and freedom as He showed Isaiah. When we live out the Call with Commitment, we will see and live out the reality which the Savior prayed for: "...Thy kingdom come. Thy will be done, as in heaven, so in earth" (Luke 11:2).

Do you believe that the whole world would benefit from coming to know the whole gospel?

_____

_____

_____

_____

Why is it important that the whole church be involved in fulfilling the whole mission?

_____

_____

_____

_____

CCD #7: CHURCH-BASED

The foundation for Christian Community Development is the Church. The affirmation of the poor and empowering them is the role God has assigned to the Church. When Paul talked about the New Testament Church, he stated in Galatians 2:8-10:

> *For God, who was at work in the ministry of Peter as an apostle to the Jews, was also at work in my ministry as an apostle to the Gentiles. James, Peter and John, those reputed to be pillars, gave me and Barnabas the right hand of fellowship when they recognized the grace given to me. They agreed that we should go to the Gentiles, and they to the Jews. All they asked was that we should continue to remember the poor, the very thing I was eager to do.*

The Church leadership was charged to go throughout the earth (the Commission Circles) and the poor must be ministered to. The relationship to the local church is the connection to God's family. Through this connection, we learn the ways of God, how to spread the love of God, and to live the life of God. Yes, our relationship with the local church gives us a spiritual accountability on earth. The local church is the place where we grow in the discipline of the life of the believer.

Why is it important that any work we do be rooted in the church?

_____

_____

_____

_____

Do you ever find it hard to love the church?

_____

_____

_____

_____

How can the Spirit help you be able to continue loving the church, even when it's hard?

_____

_____

_____

_____

The local church is at the innermost circle of the Commission Circles. While you will see the church's involvement in all the circles, it is especially highlighted here because it grows the rest of the Call. It is the local church that will influence the other rings in the Commission Circles. One cannot truly witness in the places of influence and pain without being sure-footed through a foundation solidly in the ground of truth (I Timothy 3:15). Paul provides for us the understanding of the local church in purpose and deed to live the Commission Circle through this body of Christ, Ephesians 2:14-16, 3:4-10:

For he himself is our peace, who has made the two one and has destroyed the barrier, the dividing wall of hostility, by abolishing in his flesh the law with its commandments and regulations. His purpose was to create in himself one new man out of the two, thus making peace, and in this one body to reconcile both of them to God through the cross, by which he put to death their hostility.

In reading this, then, you will be able to understand my insight into the mystery of Christ, which was not made known to people in other generations as it has now been revealed by the Spirit to God's holy apostles and prophets. This mystery is that through the gospel the Gentiles are heirs together with Israel, members together of one body, and sharers together in the promise in Christ Jesus. I became a servant of this gospel by the gift of God's grace given me through the working of his power. Although I am less than the least of all the Lord's people, this grace was given me: to preach to the Gentiles the boundless riches of Christ, and to make plain to everyone the administration of this mystery, which for ages past was kept hidden in God, who created all things. His intent was that now, through the church, the manifold wisdom of God should be made known to the rulers and authorities in the heavenly realms.

> **According to this passage, how does the church represent who Jesus is and what He has done?**

_____

_____

_____

_____

CCD #8: LISTENING TO THE COMMUNITY

Listening is key when working in communities. As I (Anthony) work in communities around the country, I tell community leaders "There is that resident that has the answer to your most pressing issue, you just haven't asked them." Or business leaders, "There is that one employee that is waiting for you to come to their desk and ask them for the answer." Or with pastors, "There is that member who is waiting for you to shake their hand and ask them about that issue, so they can give you the resolve." All this is to say, we have to reach out and listen to the communities we are called to serve.

Stop and think about the good ideas that are present in your community—or in a community in another one of the Commission Circles—that have never been heard or acted on because no one with the power to act has stopped to listen. How can you be the person who does that? How would your community change?

_____

_____

_____

_____

_____

_____

This listening should be performed with an ear to the "felt need" of the community. Instead of harping on the "wrongs" of the community, build on the "rights." Often community outsiders bring in resources without taking into account the community itself. Christian Community Development is committed to listening to the community residents, and hearing their dreams, ideas, and thoughts. This is often referred to as the "felt need" concept. Listening is most important, as the people of the community are the vested treasures of the future.

> **What is the difference between a felt need and need that someone sees from outside the community?**

_____

_____

_____

_____

_____

This listening takes on a more formal inquiry when surveys are involved. Mary Nelson makes evident this outreach to the community through "one-on-one's." She describes the approach and the questions:

> "Introduce yourself as a part of the church and indicate that you want to find out what they would like to see happen in the community.
>
> Questions to ask:
> 1) If you could wave a magic wand and make one good thing happen in the community this year, what would that be?
> 2) What talents, skills, abilities, education and experiences do you have that you think could help make this happen?
> 3) If other people had a similar vision, would you join with them to help make it happen?"[28]

Nelson discusses further, "By the time you have finished several such conversations, the possibilities for action and working together on things will become clear. After most of the interviews in adjacent communities are completed, identify the common themes of interest, and note the gifts, talents and potential leaders."[29] These questions give space for a conversation. Listening to the community creates conversations and releases potential for future actions of change. We share with leaders, both secular and faith-based, the importance of listening to impact their organizations. We label it as a "factor" in the success of leaders. Do not discredit the power of the conversations themselves, as they may well have changed the minds of those engaged.

How does the discipline of listening to the community extend honor to the people you are serving?

Listening to the communities gives us the ability to move and engage in the Commission Circles. Whether we are witnessing in family, church, community, or the tough places, listening is essential. Listening illuminates the steps of our witness. We are led by the Spirit as we are living witnesses. As we follow and are led by His spirit, listening to those we have been called to serve allows us to know where and how we can help.

> **What might keep us from listening to the community?**

_____

_____

_____

_____

> **What false beliefs about ourselves or the people we are serving might make it hard to really hear people from the community?**

_____

_____

_____

_____

To further demonstrate this, we go back to Jesus' interaction with the woman at the well. Jesus had a conversation (which is not only talking, but also listening) with the woman at the well. This conversation converted her from a skeptic to a witness. We remember when Jesus was traveling from Judea to Galilee and

CHRISTIAN COMMUNITY DEVELOPMENT

He went through Samaria (living out the Commission Circles). While there, the disciples went to get something to eat and He was left sitting on Jacob's well. (This well became the place where a Samaritan woman would encounter the Well of Life.) Jesus began a conversation with this woman of Samaria. The conversation started with Jesus asking for water, but through the exchange of ideas the conversation walked through agriculture, marriage, and religion.

Through this conversation (willingness to listen to the felt need of the woman), the woman believed and witnessed to others. John 4:39-42 shares, "Many of the Samaritans from that town believed in him because of the woman's testimony, "He told me everything I ever did." So, when the Samaritans came to him, they urged him to stay with them, and he stayed two days. And because of his words many more became believers. They said to the woman, "We no longer believe just because of what you said; now we have heard for ourselves, and we know that this man really is the Savior of the world." A collection of believers converted in Samaria (the tough place) because of one woman's conversation with someone who was willing to listen.

How can listening change lives?

_____

_____

_____

_____

We have seen and experienced how these Eight Key Components of Christian Community Development have transformed community through the power of God. We lift these components up to you, the reader, because we have seen them at work and strive to live them every day. These components lived out in homes, communities, and abroad will show the love of Christ.

EIGHT COMPONENTS OF CCD

What are the components of CCD that stand out for your ministry? Which component(s) need to be strengthened in your ministry? How will you strengthen these components?

How are these components useful in suburban ministry?
International ministry?

_____

_____

_____

_____

What leadership skill(s) do you need to develop to help
you live out the components of CCD?

_____

_____

_____

_____

What areas of CCD do you think are the biggest struggle
for you at the moment?

_____

_____

_____

_____

What areas of CCD have you seen lived out well?

_____

_____

_____

_____

_____

8   https://ccda.org/about/philosophy/

9   https://mosaicccda.com/ccd/

10   Dr. Martin Luther King, Jr.; "Propagandizing Christianity;" Sermon at Dexter Avenue Baptist Church; September 12, 1954. *[emphasis added]*

11   https://ccda.org/about/philosophy/relocation/

12   Allan Aubrey Boesak and Curtiss Paul DeYoung; Radical Reconciliation, Beyond Political Pietism and Christian Quietism; Orbis Books; 2012; page 79-80.

13   Allan Aubrey Boesak and Curtiss Paul DeYoung; Radical Reconciliation, Beyond Political Pietism and Christian Quietism; Orbis Books; 2012; Page 90.

14   https://ccda.org/about/philosophy/redistribution/ (emphasis added)

15   CCDA Institute Immersion, Chicago, April 7-12, 2013.

16   https://ccda.org/about/philosophy/leadership-development/

17   The National Center for Fathering (Fathers.com)

18   CCDA; http://www.ccda.org/about/philosophy

19   Joshua 1:1

20   Joshua 1:5 (b) KJV

21   John M. Perkins and Wayne Gordon; Leadership Revolution—Developing The Vision & Practice Of Freedom & Justice; Regal; 2012; page 143.

22   Empowerment: A Key Component of Christian Community Development, Mary Nelson, Christian Community Development Association, iUniverse, 2010, page 62, 70.

23   Robert D. Lupton, Compassion, Justice, And The Christian Life (Rethinking Ministry To The Poor), 16

24   Dr. Martin Luther King; "A Time to Break the Silence" 1967.

25   Beyond Charity: The Call to Christian Community Development, John M. Perkins, Baker Books, Jul 1, 1993 - Political Science – page 18

26   Eldin Villanfane; Beyond Cheap Grace, A Call to Radical Discipleship, Incarnation, and Justice; Wm. B. Eerdmans Publishing Co.; 2006; page 75.

27   Eldin Villanfane; Beyond Cheap Grace, A Call to Radical Discipleship, Incarnation, and Justice; Wm. B. Eerdmans Publishing Co.; 2006; page 76

28   Mary Nelson; Empowerment, A Key Component Of Christian Community Development; iUniverse; 2010; page 68.

29   Mary Nelson; Empowerment, A Key Component Of Christian Community Development; iUniverse; 2010; page 69

THE CHURCH IN ACTION:
LEADING, LIVING, LOVING,
AND LEARNING

THE COMMISSION CIRCLES AND CHRISTIAN
COMMUNITY DEVELOPMENT

WHEN FACING THE CHALLENGING PROBLEMS of our day, people are looking for an easy way. The "one, two, three" and *bam* the-community-is-fixed approach. But there are no easy solutions. The danger of outlining the commission circles or Christian Community Development like we did in Chapter 2 is that people want to run with the concept without realizing the time, effort, and work it takes to effect change.

This chapter explores how the Commission Circles are lived out in Christian Community Development. You will be disappointed if you are looking for a cookie cutter, one for one correlation between the ideas we are talking about. Again, it's not that easy; life is messy and complicated. Instead, our goal is to describe the conditions in the Circles and how some of the CCD Components are clearly demonstrated.

Why is it important to challenge cookie cutter, easy
solutions?

_____

_____

_____

_____

What resources does God give us to press into the more
complicated solutions, instead of having to stay safe with
the easy solutions?

_____

_____

_____

_____

JERUSALEM
(THE FAMILY/THE CHURCH/THE COMMUNITY)

As you remember, Jerusalem is our greatest place of influence. It is
our home, our church, our community. This is where we find the
people who interact with us the most, know us at our best (and
worst), who we can't hide from, and who we embrace.

RECONCILIATION STARTS AT HOME

If we want peace (Jerusalem being the place of peace), it has to start in the home. The American Psychological Association reports that almost 50 percent of all marriages in the United States will end in divorce or separation.[30] So flip a coin and the likelihood of you choosing heads or tails is the likelihood of Americans' success in marriage. Of course, we could hope that the divorce rates in the church will be less. Unfortunately, this is not the case; studies show that among those who identify as Christians but rarely attend church divorce rate is at 60 percent. Of those who attend church regularly, 38 percent have been divorced.[31] In order to have a better world, nation, states, cities, and communities, we have to heal our marriages and build strong families.

> **What is a practical step that you or your ministry can take to help build peace at home?**

_____

_____

_____

_____

_____

_____

LET'S PREACH JUSTICE

God is a God of justice. Better yet, God *is* Justice: one of the names of God is 'Elohei mishpat, which means God of Justice. Isaiah shares with us the desires of a just God, "Yet the Lord longs to be gracious to you; therefore, he will rise up to show you compassion. For the Lord is a God of justice" (Isaiah 30:18).

How does the church reflect justice? Is there room for grace? Compassion? If God is about justice, why don't we hear justice preached about in the pulpit? The modern-day church has relegated justice to being an enemy of capitalism, and therefore an enemy of God. Because unfortunately, capitalism moved from being a system of commerce to influencing the way the gospel is taught across our country every Sunday morning.

> Sometimes people think of justice and spiritual health as being almost opposite goals, but God holds both of these together in Himself. What does it mean to serve a God of justice and of righteousness?

_____

_____

_____

_____

_____

_____

If our Gospel doesn't demonstrate both God as Justice and God as Holy, then something is wrong with our Gospel. How have you seen God in both ways?

_____

_____

_____

_____

Why do you think there is a tendency to emphasize just one aspect of God's character and to neglect the other part(s)?

_____

_____

_____

_____

Just like God distributes resources spiritually and naturally, He gives to His people so that they can redistribute what they have been given. Pastor John admits this when he sees it in himself—confessing "I really don't love until I want for my neighbor what I want for myself." This type of preaching plays a prophetic role in shifting our focus from the old adage, "getting all I can, and canning what I get" to caring for those who are without and working to share the resources we have. This other way is the New Testament model of the church: Acts 2:44-45, "All the believers were together and had everything in common. They sold property and possessions to give to anyone who had need."

The church has lost its voice; the presence of leading. The Civil Rights Movement was led by the church. Led by a minister. Now, in a time where we need leaders, we have been relegated to lead the people in the pew but not the community where we worship. The kingdom here on earth will be realized block by block, corner by corner, street by street. Seeking justice to solve the inequity of resources. Peace in the pulpit, lived in our homes, walked in the streets. Honoring and seeing a just God.

> **What are the needs of justice in today's world where the voice of the church could lead people not only to freedom, but also to spiritual health?**

Do you think spiritual health is possible without justice?

_____

_____

_____

_____

_____

_____

LISTEN, LISTEN, LISTEN

Even though we are emphasizing the important role that you have in the community, there should also be a word of warning to practitioners: we are not the answers. We are not the solutions. We are not the heroes. **We are servants.** Servants who must listen in order to understand the needs of those we are called to serve. Not this idea of "let's hurry up and fix it and move on," but instead staying engaged and, in love, learning the "felt needs" of the community.

Dr. Perkins clearly outlines the importance of addressing felt needs and the danger of not spending time understanding in his book _Beyond Charity: The Call to Christian Community Development_.[32] Some practitioners have trained for so long that they are ready for action and see listening as non-activity. But listening _is_ activity. Listening is the only way we can truly understand, know, and gain the credibility needed in order to be a part of the community and improve communities.

> How can you and your ministry learn to "count" listening
> as a useful and meaningful activity?

_____

_____

_____

_____

_____

This activity of listening and observing is Biblical. God gave Ezekiel a picture of the people of Israel rising from dry bones to become a great army (Ezekiel 37). Ezekiel, the "preacher practitioner," did not start by preaching, he started by observing and listening. Ezekiel 37:1-2: "The hand of the Lord was on me, and he brought me out by the Spirit of the Lord and set me in the middle of a valley; it was full of bones. He led me back and forth among them, and I saw a great many bones on the floor of the valley, bones that were very dry." Ezekiel was able to give an assessment of the situation because he was around the people, interacting with them, listening to them.

We practitioners further receive wise counsel from Ezekiel as God asks him a pointed question. Ezekiel 37:3: "He asked me, "Son of man, can these bones live?" Ezekiel did not tout his years in seminary, leadership conferences, or experiences. Neither did Ezekiel tell God how dry the bones were and the impossibility of the situation. Ezekiel answered as we should as we serve in community, "Sovereign Lord, you alone know." God alone is supreme and has ultimate authority, we are wise when we lean on His word.

> How can listening to the community point us (and the community) back to God?

_____

_____

_____

_____

_____

_____

LIVE WHERE YOU MAKE IMPACT

What better example of relocation is there than Jesus Christ? The Message translation of the Holy Scripture gives us a view of His relocation, John 1:14, "The Word became flesh and blood, and moved into the neighborhood. We saw the glory with our own eyes, the one-of-a-kind glory, like Father, like Son, Generous inside and out, true from start to finish." What a beautiful sight!

What more are we to do today!?!? The church is to be Jesus in the hood. It is the idea of incarnational ministry. Not people coming into the neighborhood, doing church, and then going back home. It is living out the call of God by living and worshiping among the underserved.

Like the principle of redistribution, it is seen in Acts 2:44-45, "All the believers were together and had everything in common. They sold property and possessions to give to anyone who had need." The church worships together, fellowships together, and cares for one another's needs. When we do this, the world sees Jesus here among us.

> Do your neighbors know that God has moved into our human neighborhood? How can you help them know that? How can the church help them to know it?

_____

_____

_____

_____

_____

JERUSALEM—GOD IN THE HOOD

I, John, believe that one of the hardest parts of living out this form of ministry (CCD) is choosing to live among the poor. While it is tough to do, it is even tougher for those who have been brought up to believe that success means moving away from the neighborhood. The narrative has to change, and we need to demonstrate the Jesus model.

Why might it be harder for someone to remain in their community of need than for someone else to relocate there from the outside?

_____

_____

_____

_____

Jesus came down from heaven and lived among us. The term often used is "incarnational." He did not stay in heaven to preach, teach, heal, and save. No, Jesus came among us and showed us what justice looked like. We also must move among those who have been marginalized to minister effectively. Our ministry starts in our homes, our schools, our churches, our neighborhoods. We live justice when we truly desire for our neighbors the same things we desire for ourselves.

Do you see your church (and yourself) learning to want the same things for your neighbors that you want for yourselves?

_____

_____

_____

_____

How does this change when you move into a community with high needs?

_____

_____

_____

_____

_____

Why is it sometimes tempting not to want for our neighbors what we want for ourselves?

_____

_____

_____

_____

_____

All that being said, even with years of my family living, ministering, and sharing in the neighborhood, I don't feel that we actually became a part of the neighborhood until we put our children in public schools. We had our children in private schools in an effort to keep our children away from "them" (those in the neighborhood whose parents were not educated, who have been marginalized, and who are poor). We had a perfectly good school right near the house, and one day we decided to move them from the private school to the nearby public school.

Then it started. We had the same interest of the school succeeding as our neighbors because our children were there. I didn't come to the school to see about the other's kids. No, I wanted to check to see if my kids were learning, being cared for, and had access to the best. But my concern for my kids helps make the school better for everyone. We have an enhanced understanding—that living among those we are called to minister to is taken to another level when we are vested in the community's success. For us it was the schools, for others it may be investing in the housing market that gives them a closer connection to the development of the area. For someone else it might be owning a local business that will call him or her to care about the zoning and codes in the area. Ministry in Jerusalem is investing beyond just church; it is caring for the people and living conditions surrounding the church by being present in the community.

> **Think about Jesus. How did he demonstrate what it looks like to want for others what we want for ourselves?**

JUDEA (CITYWIDE IMPACT)

Our church has to impact our cities. The New Testament church went underground while still preaching, teaching, and worshipping. Their impact was felt in Judea. Now we have churches on every corner and little to no impact on our city. The cities are the central ground of many of the things we are struggling with as a society. The church must be the hands and feet of Jesus to effect change.

LEADERSHIP DEVELOPMENT—THE ART OF DISCIPLESHIP

Sadly, most churches have relegated leadership development to focusing on the youth. No one will argue against children being the future and the importance of their development (we further explore the importance of youth development later in the book), but we also must develop the "leaders of the now". Investing in youth will see results in years, investing in adults can result in seeing changes today. But investing in adults is tough. We are willing to deal with children because they don't know any better. When we deal with adults, we feel they should know better and even look down on them because they don't know better. We have to stop this belittling of people. We cannot love and demonize at the same time.

How can we be churches that develop both youth and today's adults, instead of favoring one group over the other?

_____

_____

_____

_____

How is focusing on leadership development among today's adults important for the growth and health of today's youth?

_____

_____

_____

_____

_____

The church has to get back to discipleship at all ages and stages. Walking with others and sharing with them as Christ becomes the foundation of their lives. What else should the church be doing? Of course, the answer is, *a lot*! But what else should be at the core of leadership development? Nothing. Jesus discipled twelve adults and changed the world!

Working with others to lead out of the love of Christ, and living with them as they learn those tools, is discipleship and leadership development:

The important distinction with Christian discipleship is that we are not only called to learn the teachings of Jesus Christ, we are also called to live them. A disciple who bases his or her life on the teachings of Christ [is] "like a person building a house, who dug a deep hole to lay the foundation on rock" (Luke 6:48). When we make our initial declaration of faith and ask Christ to be our Savior, He will begin changing us from the inside, giving us the ability to understand His word and the desire to live it.[33]

This type of leadership development is seen when Jesus teaches us about the farmer who sowed seeds and later reaped the harvest. You remember, the farmer goes out and sows seeds. There were varying conditions of the soil (people's abilities to produce) and varying events that occurred (circumstances of life), but at the end of the day there was a harvest. Something came out that was good. As we feed into future leaders, there will be some success and some failure. Most importantly, we are strong to live like Jesus and striving to invite others to a life with Him.

Even being the master disciple-maker He was, one of His followers was a devil. Like Jesus, we will have some who will fail. And also like Jesus, we will have some who will carry the gospel and grow in grace.

How can expecting a mix of success and failure help us to keep up the work of discipleship?

_____

_____

_____

_____

What does it look like for you to model being a disciple while you help other people also move toward discipleship?

_____

_____

_____

_____

What is the connection between discipling and equipping members of the church?

_____

_____

_____

_____

MY BROTHER'S KEEPER

There are, today, churches who have all the resources they need. They have no lack of funding, people, and influence to advance the kingdom. At the same time, there are churches that are under-resourced. They have little money, few who attend, and minimal impact. Sometimes these churches—so different from each other—are only a few blocks apart from each other. This dispensation of resources can be balanced through redistribution of funding, people, and influence so the kingdom can be realized on every block.

Redistribution in the sense we are advocating is not about welfare or merely sending money. We are talking about partnerships of mutual benefit to see the work of God accomplished. God's intention for all His children to be saved and served should not be hampered because of the inequity of an economic system. It must be overcome by the love of Christ in us working together and sharing for all of us to see the kingdom.

We cannot be stuck on sending money to a sister church in the "hood" and call it good. That is no better than any other money-only redistribution system. What we are talking about is about living together. Working together. Fellowshipping together. Seeing my brother as my responsibility. I (Anthony) saw this when I was a part of a men's fellowship that met weekly. Two of the guys who had been studying the Bible together for months ran into each other at the city dump. They start talking and one recently was released from prison and had started cleaning out buildings to earn money. The other had a construction business for years. Their kinship earned in studying the word together created a partnership that was mutually beneficial economically. Stories like this are happening all over the country. It is not by chance, but by the design of intentional sharing and redistribution.

> It can be tempting to look at those who have less than us and assume that it is "their fault" and so we can even convince ourselves that we wouldn't honor the Lord by sharing our resources with them. How does this approach match with the ideas just discussed?

_____

_____

_____

_____

> What does a "poor" church have to give to a "rich" church?

_____

_____

_____

JUDEA—IMPACTING THE CITY

The disciples in the book of Acts had to be pushed out of Jerusalem through suffering and persecution. I (John) don't know what will push the Church out of its comfort zone in our day, but we can't make a difference in the city without real relationships. We have to get out of our comfort zones and be willing to fellowship with others. In this context I often wonder whether blacks and whites ever have true friendship.

I remember a church planting meeting that I attended in the city. I was bothered because there was no talk of justice and reconciliation. I was even more annoyed that it seemed that no one respected me as a fellow church planter. No one greeted me, shook my hand, or even acknowledged my presence. After every meeting, I signed up on the email list and never received an email invitation. I kept attending because I knew someone who was a part of the church. Finally, I stopped, knowing that these people did not desire my participation in their work.

I tell all my friends that I know that I have true reconciliation in Common Ground Church when I see Mississippi whites willing to worship with us. City impact—impact in Judea—is in this space where we start dealing with one another. This will lead to the Samaria experience.

> **What difficult step is the Lord calling you to? Or what difficult step has He already called you to?**

> What does the Gospel have to say about reaching across groups—even groups that we have prejudices against?

_____

_____

_____

SAMARIA
(SERVING IN THE PLACES OF CONFLICT)

Samaria symbolizes the place where there is tension, greatest need, and where it is hardest to work. Here's what we should know about Jesus' trip to Samaria:

He must needs go through Samaria—i.e., following the shortest and most usual road, and the one we find Him taking from Galilee to Jerusalem (Luke 9:52 . . .). Josephus spoke of this as the customary way of the Galileans going up during the feasts at Jerusalem . . . . The Pharisees, indeed, took the longer road through Peræa, to avoid contact with the country and people of Samaria, but it is within the purpose of His life and work ("needs go," i.e., was necessary that He should go) to teach in Samaria, as in Judæa, the principles of true religion and worship, which would cut away the foundations of all local jealousies and feuds, and establish for all nations the spiritual service of the universal Father (John 4:21-24).[34]

SAMARIA—PLACE OF GREATEST NEED AND GREATEST OPPORTUNITY

Jesus obviously saw the need to go to Samaria and, as we discussed before, we see Him having a conversation with a woman at a well. Their conversation ranges from marital status, to race, to worship, to water. This conservation that Jesus had with one woman leads to a citywide evangelistic meeting. The woman runs back to the men in the city and does not talk about marriage, race, worship or water. She says, "Come, see a man, which told me all things that ever I did: is not this the Christ?"[35] After meeting Jesus, the men tell her, "We no longer believe just because of what you said; now we have heard for ourselves, and we know that this man really is the Savior of the world."[36]

Just like Jesus' work in Samaria, we are called to these places known for the conflict, tension, and misunderstanding. As these places are turned around for Christ, many will be saved. Our focus may be on one, but He can save many. The Apostles were driven out of Jerusalem and sought safety in Samaria. From the seeds Jesus planted, they reaped a harvest from His work.

Do you find yourself resisting the call to Samaria? Why or why not?

_____

_____

_____

_____

SAMARIA IS NOT GOD-FORSAKEN NOR GOD-FORGOTTEN

We must be careful not to misjudge these "tough, marginalized, under-resourced" places to be God-forsaken or forgotten. We must be careful not to think that when we arrive in these areas, God arrives, as if God is not already there. It was not readily apparent to the Apostles that there were believers in Samaria, but believers were there, and they provided safety for the them. As practitioners, we cannot go into these places assuming God is not working. He is not only working, but He is providing for them in His way. We cannot allow our arrogance to blind us to the work of God.

> It is common for short term missions teams to talk about how they are going to take Jesus to the place they are going to visit. What is right and wrong with this idea?

BRICKS WITHOUT STRAW

It is not enough on to address injustice at its edges, but it must be addressed at its systemic core. When we are willing to redistribute our influence to those who are underserved, we cannot ignore the unjust economic, judicial, employment, and housing systems they live with. Dr. Martin Luther King, Jr. said, "It's all right to tell a man to lift himself by his own bootstraps, but it is a cruel jest to say to a bootless man that he ought to lift himself by his own bootstraps."[37]

We still hear this "bootstrap" theory to addressing injustice today. It is especially cruel when we continue to feed the systems that widen the cavern between the haves and have nots. Redistribution closes the gap. This is about ensuring that my brother can make a living wage to buy the boots. We must make sure he has the skills to lift himself from where he is to where he wants to be without the impediments of substandard boots.

> How does living in close proximity to people, and listening to the community, help us to understand what justice and injustice look like in their lives?

The United States Farm Bill is an example of how systems can be set up to ensure success of our citizens. The first farm bill was passed during the Great Depression to provide financial assistance to farmers suffering from the low prices of food because of the excess of crops. Later farmers were paid not to farm, and the government paid farmers for excess grain. A food stamp program was also set up to ensure a steady market that farmers could depend on. It was decided that the free market should govern agriculture in America and farms then had to take out low interest loans if they ran into issues. At the same time, direct annual government assistance was given to farmers based on yield and acreage over the last 10 years. While we are not trying to say this is the best system, this is an example of how the government will step in and support what we deem as important.

What better place to invest in than the underserved places in America? Not what we are seeing around the country, where places are cleaned up and people are moved out. But investing in those living in the communities and allowing those who have lived there to continue to live there and benefit from the bettering of neighborhood.

> Government programs usually carry both some risk and some benefit—but it is interesting to look at our attitudes about different kinds of programs. If your church favors some programs and not others, what is underneath those judgments? If we favor programs that benefit people like us and not those that benefit people different from us, how does that connect to loving our neighbor as ourselves?

THE CHURCH AS THE FOCAL POINT OF COMMUNITY

If caring for the least and the lost is living out the gospel, we must find ourselves living, suffering, and advocating for change among those we are called to serve. We want to move from being churches in the neighborhood with closed doors and hearts, to being neighbors loving, worshipping, and living with one another. We want a place where the church strives to meet the needs the neighbor rather than the neighbors fulfilling the needs of the church. Not outreach to pull others in, but living out the will of God so others want to experience the worshipping of the God who loves us all.

> What would it look like for your church to demonstrate the will and character of God in a way your neighbors can understand?

_____

_____

_____

_____

_____

The church has to be the place where issues are solved. If there is a need for better housing, who else but the chosen of God should pull the resources together to build affordable housing and transition our neighbors from renters to homeowners? What is better than that the church should teach the biblical intent of financing starting with giving back to God and being good stewards of the rest? Why should not the church be establishing enterprises to employ neighbors (with an eye to developing entrepreneurs), sharing the love of God along with skills and fiscal resources to uplift the financial status of poor communities?

> **Do you think of your church as the place where issues are solved? Why or why not? How have you seen this lived out?**

_____

_____

_____

_____

_____

When we live among the people, we can start to see the needs for system changing institutions launched from the love of God. Common Ground Lawn-Care is just one of those businesses created to fight against the adverse effects of the prison system. Pastor John tells the story:

> We had so many members who had a prison record in our community and we wanted to do something to ensure they had some income. I was looking at all the overgrown properties in the neighborhood and I knew that we could make our living space beautiful. I got a couple of lawn mowers, weed eaters, a truck, some gas and we started to work. Two years later we have hired one manager from the West Jackson

Community as well as continuing to run a crew of 2 people from the neighborhood. We are working at over 40 properties (including one with the city of Jackson), and we are making money. What a winning combination!?!?! Look at the power of God!

> **The church is intended to be an agent of change in the world—how does this play out in your community?**

THE ENDS OF THE EARTH (TO THE ENDS OF THE EARTH: MINISTERING IN THE MARGINS)

While we understand that Jesus desires to reach every end of the globe with the Good News, we also understand that this goal is impossible for one person, organization, ministry or church. But how about ensuring everyone within your sphere is reached? How about ensuring that our churches don't only minister to those who look like us, eat like us, drive what we drive, read the same things we do? How about caring for the forgotten, the overlooked, those who have been given up on? Could Jesus expect that of us? The answer is a resounding, "Yes!"

How would your community look different if everyone
had the opportunity to know Jesus?

_____

_____

_____

_____

_____

_____

There are some communities where almost no one has access to the message of Jesus. Does your church (or do you)
have a responsibility to respond to this need?

_____

_____

_____

_____

_____

_____

How can your church and ministry impact the world at all four levels: Jerusalem, Judea, Samaria, and to the Ends of the Earth?

_____

_____

_____

_____

_____

Jesus teaches about the Kingdom of Heaven and shares the care we should show to all; when we fulfill His will in others, we are doing it to Him. Matthew 25:37-40 says: "Then the righteous will answer him, 'Lord, when did we see you hungry and feed you, or thirsty and give you something to drink? When did we see you a stranger and invite you in, or needing clothes and clothe you? When did we see you sick or in prison and go to visit you?' The King will reply, 'Truly I tell you, whatever you did for one of the least of these brothers and sisters of mine, you did for me.'" The fulfilling of the gospel is ministering in the margins.

Now that we have established a framework to lead from, the next chapters will discuss how this framework is lived out and our experiences. Leading, living, loving, and learning in community is not easy, but are essential for the light of Christ to be seen on earth. Our efforts on the following pages tell how to move beyond the theoretical to the practical.

What is your "Jerusalem, Judea, and Samaria"?

_____

_____

_____

_____

_____

_____

What are you doing to affect the world?

_____

_____

_____

_____

_____

_____

_____

What do your partners, community, and other stakeholders say you are doing to address their needs? Does their
assessment align with your views of ministering in "Jerusalem, Judea, and Samaria"? What changes can you make
to align with their expectations? Should your activities
align more with their expectations (why or why not)?

30   https://www.apa.org/topics/divorce/

31   Bradley R.E. Wright, Christians Are Hate-Filled Hypocrites … and Other Lies
You've Been Told, (Minneapolis, MN: Bethany House, 2010), p. 133.

32   Beyond Charity: The Call to Christian Community Development. John M.
Perkins 1993

33   https://www.allaboutfollowingjesus.org/discipleship-definition.htm

34   https://biblehub.com/commentaries/john/4-4.htm Ellicott's Commentary for
English Readers

35   John 4:29 KJV

36   John 4:41-42

37   King, Martin Luther, Jr. (March 31, 1968). "Remaining Awake Through a Great
Revolution" Delivered at the National Cathedral, Washington, D.C.

LEADING IN PRACTICE

AS WE DISCUSSED IN THE last chapter, the Commission Circles concept does not lead to some clean program that you can pick up and drop into any community. We are talking about an approach that changes the way we think about the community and what it means to live the presence of Jesus there. In this chapter we want to talk about the ways this plays out in real life. So, in the Commission Circles, we share where to minister. The components of Christian Community Development give us guides for how to minister. Jesus' first sermon gives us clear areas to minister in (Luke 4:18-19):

> *"The Spirit of the Lord is on me, because he has anointed me to proclaim good news to the poor. He has sent me to proclaim freedom for the prisoners and recovery of sight for the blind, to set the oppressed free, to proclaim the year of the Lord's favor."*

As we examine ministering in the margins, let's see how Christ outlines His ministry.

LUKE 4:18: PROCLAIM THE GOOD NEWS:

COFFEESHOP CHRISTIANITY

Before we go any further, we want to explain what will be obvious to some, but to be true to ourselves we must make it clear. There is a difference between "ministering *in* the margins" and "ministering *to* the margins." Ministering *to* the margins is this coffeeshop Christianity, meaning we meet in comfortable places, drink coffee, and make plans for those people.

Ministering to the margins is posting online and gaining followers, but with no change in the neighborhood. Ministering in the margins means getting your hands dirty. It means things will not go right, and we will continue to work and give. Our mentor and friend Reverend Matthew Watts, Pastor of Grace Bible Church of Charlestown, WV, calls ministering *in* the margins true "restorative justice." He points to the text Matthew 5:38-42:

> *You have heard that it was said, 'Eye for eye, and tooth for tooth.' But I tell you, do not resist an evil person. If anyone slaps you on the right cheek, turn to them the other cheek also. And if anyone wants to sue you and take your shirt, hand over your coat as well. If anyone forces you to go one mile, go with them two miles. Give to the one who asks you, and do not turn away from the one who wants to borrow from you.*

This high bar of ministry is the call for followers of Christ.

> **How can you move toward ministry *in* the margins, rather than just *to* the margins?**

_____

_____

_____

_____

> **Describe a time you have seen this done well.**

_____

_____

_____

_____

FAMILY FIRST: WHAT DO YOU GUYS THINK?

We (John and Anthony) are often asked, "If you could only focus on one thing, what would that be?" Our response is always "family." Of course, that question is not fair. It tries to take life, which is complicated and messy, and act as if there is a simple fix. Meanwhile, we believe a commitment to family is essential to growing communities.

Ministering in the margins is done at its best when we positively affect families. If we want to change the generations of evil that have thrived in so many communities, we have to start turning around the beliefs, habits, and activities of the family.

Consider the following thoughts: "Single parent families are ideal," "Prison records are just the way of life," or "Because we have not had it in the past, we do not deserve it now." These ideals are signs of an unhealthy community. No one should judge those of us in these situations, but we must continue to offer support and to expose others to a different way of life. When ministering in communities armed with the grace of God, we cannot ignore the social and moral ills that create the many challenges.

Again, we share the thoughts of Reverend Watts and what he calls "the unwavering focus on family and youth development." The rebuilding of the family (in whatever manner that looks like in our community) is important. Watts further shares that this is a biblical principle: "God always tied the promise to the parent's seed [children]. He would give *generational* promises, your children's, children's, children will be blessed. So, whether it is Adam, Abraham, or Noah, God told them things would be better through their lineage" (emphasis added). This is not only an Old Testament concept, but we see the gospel of Matthew starts with the generations of Jesus, connecting even the son of God to family.

According to Watts, this unwavering focus on family and youth development "ties the parents to the children." It prevents us from wasting our time, treasure, and resources on ourselves. Instead, we invest in the children and in their future. We have lost this focus on future investment along with the tie between parents and children. Many people believe that today is all that matters. However, rebuilding the family will strengthen our communities, and we will become the village again—caring for each other as family.

> **List three practical steps you can take toward healthy family.**

_____

_____

_____

_____

_____

LET THE CHILDREN COME

One of the concerning actions of Christ's disciples is their response to the children in Matthew 19:13. We wish we could just go back and ask them, "What are you thinking?" Matthew 19:13-15 states:

Then people brought little children to Jesus for him to place his hands on them and pray for them. But the disciples rebuked them.

Jesus said, "Let the little children come to me, and do not hinder them, for the kingdom of heaven belongs to such as these." When he had placed his hands on them, he went on from there.

Investing in our youth is well worth it. Consider the countless stories of people who gave their lives to Christ through a Good News Club or AWANA. Both of us were brought up with spiritual nurturing through Sunday School and Christian youth programs that made us the men we are today.

We must continue to support these programs. We have to adapt our traditional methods of engaging our youth to ensure we are engaging them with today's technology while telling them the same old story of the Savior of the world. We also need to ensure these programs infuse skills that prepare them to be successful adults. Not "successful" as the world defines it but allowing them the space to explore Christ in church, work, and home. This means teaching financial literacy from a Biblical perspective, ways to handle conflict as a Christian, and methods for healthy, loving relationships with Christ at the center. We cannot expect the world to teach our children these things in a Christian manner. It must come from the Church of God.

What can you do to help your church or ministry serve both kids and adults well?

_____

_____

_____

_____

NO KID IS AN ISLAND

As we discussed in the previous chapter, many times we are willing to embrace and work with the children, but we ignore their surroundings. What are we doing for the parents and/or guardians of these children? We usually have the attitude, "Well, they should know better." Then we act as if the children we are investing in do not see how we treat their caregivers. This is, at most, mistreatment and, at the least, disregard. It is not helpful to the growth and development of the child.

The components of Christian Community Development aid in helping us care, not only for the child, but their surroundings. The schools, the parks, and the corner store all play a role in the growth of the child. Limiting our programs to just the child is short-sighted and ill-advised.

(W)holistic ministry means that we have to pay attention to people in their contexts. How can you use the principles of CCD to move beyond ministering to the individual into ministering to the whole community?

_____

_____

_____

_____

_____

EXPOSE NOT EXPLOIT

With much dismay, John and I (Anthony) have talked about the many times we get a call from the office of some political figure asking us to get our kids together to attend this or that event. Unfortunately, these events are little more than a photo opportunity. They call us so they can get our black and brown children's faces on camera, feed them, and send them back to the neighborhood until the next event when they need to appear to be connected to the community.

We are not saying we should not answer and respond positively to the request, but we should ask for more than a picture and a meal. In order for things to change and for policies for our children to be considered, we need advocates. We wish we had asked for a continued liaison in the mayor's office. Or that they genuinely consider a policy that we drafted with the community. Or even respond to a request for funding a sustaining program, activity, or project. We should take opportunities to let people see our children, and at the same time push the agenda to better our community.

We will go more in-depth on the need for the church to enter in the realm of public policy on the following pages, but here we want to mention how some are teaching the Bible in school because of state legislation. A Christian group is pushing Bible classes in public schools. The Washington Post published an article on May 10, 2019, entitled "A conservative Christian group is pushing Bible classes in public schools nationwide—and it's working." This article shares this wave of enlightenment that is brightening our country. "Scenes of Bible classes in public school could become increasingly common across the United States if other states follow Kentucky's lead in passing legislation that encourages high schools to teach the Bible," states the article.

"Activists on the religious right, through their legislative effort Project Blitz, drafted a law that encourages Bible classes in public schools and persuaded at least ten state legislatures to introduce versions of it this year. Georgia and Arkansas recently passed bills that are awaiting their governors' signatures." Teaching the Bible in school, what a novel idea! Unfortunately, our recent history in America has pushed the teaching of religion out of the schools; therefore, we have a generation in America who have not been exposed to the Bible (not even as a book of literature, much less as the Word of God). Let's not watch, but participate, in revitalizing the teachings of the Bible in our schools.

How can you advocate for the wellbeing of those that you have responsibility for?

LUKE 4:18: PROCLAIM THE GOOD NEWS TO THE POOR

CARING FOR THE POOR

Yes, we are the church. Yes, there is a separation between church and state. Yes, there is a role for the church, and there is a role for government. We should not allow the line between church and state to lead us to believe the church should not be involved with public policy, especially in caring for the poor.

The church has always been in the forefront of public policy. We think about the leading and supporting efforts of the 19th century leader Sojourner Truth in the Abolitionist and Women's Rights Movements. Her efforts led to the 13th and the 19th Amendments, ending slavery and giving women the right to vote respectively. What would the Civil Rights Movement be without the leadership of Reverend Martin Luther King, Jr., ending segregation in public places, banning employment discrimination on the basis of race, color, religion, sex or national origin, and resulting in the passing of the 14th and 15th Amendment? The church did not and should not sit back and be apathetic to needed changes in policies, especially when those changes can better the conditions of those in the margins.

There are a few prophetic voices, who are not only preaching in the pulpit, but also marching in the streets and knocking on doors for public policy addressing poverty. Reverend William J. Barber II has been in the forefront of addressing issues of the poor for years. The pastor of Greenleaf Christian Church (Disciples of Christ) in Goldsboro, North Carolina, and the president of the

North Carolina National Association for the Advancement of Colored People (NAACP), Barber has taken a page out the Dr. King's playbook and is introducing a new "Poor People's Campaign". He writes:

> Still, we have never completed the Reconstruction that our federal government admitted was necessary after the Civil War. Just as the Poor People's Campaign proposed, the Reconstruction we need now must arise from the efforts of people harmed directly by racism, poverty, environmental degradation, and the war economy. That is the inspiration for the new Poor People's Campaign: A National Call for Moral Revival, which is coordinating direct actions across the country that will begin in May [2019]. Activists in at least 32 states and Washington, D.C., will join in 40 days of civil disobedience, including an encampment in the nation's capital, in hopes of building the power of the poor and the working class to reset the national agenda.[38]

The church must learn from the mistakes of the past. We cannot do what we did in the 1960's. While many members of the church got involved with the Civil Rights Movement, many more sat on the sidelines or even criticized its methods and motives. No movement is perfect. Both those of us who lead and those of us who follow are flawed. We should not allow these failures in us to outweigh the need for God to work through us to get things done. For the greater good, we must act now, get involved, and set a new paradigm of engagement despite our imperfection.

Public policy is a really hard area for the church. What has the church done well? What challenges are there? How might Jesus be calling us beyond what we are comfortable with?

_____

_____

_____

_____

_____

LUKE 4:18: PROCLAIM FREEDOM

PUBLIC POLICY FOR THOSE IN THE MARGINS HAS PROVEN TO HELP EVERYONE

I, Anthony, have been involved in public policy for more than 27 years. The implementation of the Americans with Disabilities Act (ADA, signed by George H.W. Bush in 1990) showed me how public policy, when developed for those who are challenged in our society, helps all in society. Who doesn't use a rolling suitcase and find the ramp leading to the building more convenient than lifting the bag up the stairs? Who has not used the voice activated commands on their electronic devices? Or increased the size of the text in their electronic document for ease of use? These life conveniences were made possible, whether directly or indirectly through the ADA.

All public facilities around the nation must comply with the ADA. This law was aimed at making it possible for those with "disabilities" to have "normal" function in society, it actually served the whole society. It made more facilities, functions, and activities available to more people.

This idea—that helping a "challenged" part of society provides greater access to the entire society—has held true in other public policies. Businesses tout the importance of diversity, and then bottom lines and creativity increase. The Forbes article, "Embracing Diversity and Fostering Inclusion Is Good for Your Business," demonstrates our point when it says, "Diversity and inclusion are topics on many executive agendas. Companies should be working to create more diversity within and outside of their organization, because firstly, it's the right thing to do, and secondly, it makes business sense. Companies in the top quartile for gender diversity outperform their competitors by 15% and those in the top quartile for ethnic diversity outperform their competitors by 35%."[39] Some of the same businesses that thought it was evil to hire minorities and woman and believed the government policy was an overreach, now benefit from the increased profits of employing "those" people.

We believe the same thing can happen as we address poverty through public policy. It has been difficult to get the attention of legislators. Many feel the government should not deal with the poor through policy and that this should be the role of philanthropic institutions. Businesses see this as "anti-capitalism" (as expressed toward raising the minimum wage). Like the challenges that were encountered when addressing other issues of those marginalized, addressing poverty will better our democracy and allow more people the pursuit of happiness. Good policy provides the structure to support a better life.

How can solidarity with your neighbor end up bringing greater good for the whole community?

LUKE 4:18: SET THE OPPRESSED FREE

INCARCERATION

We understand that most of the readers of this type of book are well familiar with the incarceration rates in the U.S. and its racial makeup. But for those who are not aware of this issue and why we feel it needs to be addressed, here are some statistics.

Bureau of Justice Statistics, Prisoners in 2017 Summary Report:

> *At year-end 2017, more than twice as many white females (49,100 prisoners) were in state and federal prisons as black (19,600) or Hispanic (19,400) females. However, the rate*

for black females in prison per 100,000 black females in the population was almost double that for white females (92 per 100,000 black female U.S. residents compared to 49 per 100,000 white female U.S. residents). The imprisonment rate was 66 per 100,000 Hispanic females.

At the end of 2016, an estimated 60% of Hispanics and blacks in state prison had been sentenced for a violent offense, compared to 48% of white prisoners. The Bureau of Justice Statistics Prisoners in 2017 imprisonment rate of sentenced black adults declined by 4% from 2016 to 2017 and by 31% from 2007 to 2017. However, at year-end 2017, the imprisonment rate for sentenced black males (2,336 per 100,000 black male U.S. residents) was almost six times that of sentenced white males (397 per 100,000 white male U.S. residents).[40]

This direct quote from the Bureau of Justice Statistics presents the information as if there is some hope because "more than twice as many white females" are imprisoned than Blacks and Hispanics, or because the "imprisonment rate of sentenced black adults declined by 4%…" These seemingly hopeful statistics are then qualified with a "however" and then give way to hopelessness. Our focus is not to argue against an unjust system or Americans' over obsession with imprisonment (especially when it comes to blacks and browns). There are great books dealing with this issue like Michelle Alexander's, *The New Jim Crow* or our friend Dominique DuBois Gilliard's book *Rethinking Incarceration: Advocating for Justice that Restores.*

There is a need for the church to accept the opportunity to turn these statistics around by giving chances to those who have made mistakes. What better way to demonstrate "freedom for the prisoners" than giving them tools to never be imprisoned again? Notice we say the tools because just like any other situation, life is about choices. We believe the church must give opportunities that will break the cycle of recidivism.

> Some people might say that these are not issues for the church, while others would say that they clearly are issues for the church. Paul says that Christians are supposed to care about each other more than they care about them-selves (Philippians 2). How might that passage impact our understanding of an issue like mass incarceration?

_____

_____

_____

_____

_____

_____

POWER TO GET WEALTH

Before we discuss how we believe everyone should have oppor-tunities, we have to address "prosperity preaching." Prosperity preaching says things like if you "turn around 3 times, God's gonna bless you" or "bring $500 to the altar, you will get your blessing by Wednesday." This type of preaching is the same thing the state does when they get so many of the poor to buy lottery tickets. It plays on the trust and beliefs that people have in God to seemingly exploit them. This is not biblical; this is not godly.

Why do you think magical thinking, like prosperity preaching, is attractive to people in need?

_____

_____

_____

_____

_____

On the other hand, some of the biggest critics of "prosperity preaching" are financially secure and it is easy for them to look down on those who believe in God to provide in the area of money. These critics are not unbelievers like Karl Marx, German philosopher and economist, who said "Religion is the opium of the people."[41] These are Christians who don't criticize the belief in the healing power of God when their loved one is sick. They don't mind believing in a God for deliverance when they need their loved one to get off drugs. Is belief in God only for things we can't get in our own power?

What do people in your community trust God for?

_____

_____

_____

_____

_____

While the "prosperity preaching" is dangerous and harmful, it is just as dangerous for us not to demonstrate justice in our lives. It is just as harmful for us not believe in a God who can provide, even in the financial and material world. Let's not stand back and judge, when our strength can be to offer opportunity, wisdom, and resources to those in need. We should not sentence one to a lifetime of poverty because of our misconceived notions of their worth, theology, or ability.

I (Anthony) have done some work with Andre Smalley, president and owner of Truly Solar (Upper Marlboro, Maryland) in the area of staff development. The combination of the chance to pour into other entrepreneurs, the opportunity to see an organization grow, and the belief everyone can be successful while saving the planet makes the work with Andre one of my most rewarding experiences.

Truly Solar's mission is to place control of your source of electricity in the hands of customers and to make the ability to control the electricity one needs, while making it as affordable as possible.

Oh, by the way, Truly Solar is African American owned and they intentionally believe in giving people another chance (even those who have been incarcerated). Andre explains his workforce philosophy this way: "From my experience, many of these individuals we hire were in jail for selling drugs. We just give them a legal product to use those skills to sell."

While Truly Solar is not a ministry or connected to a church, it is a case study of going beyond providing those who have made mistakes a living wage, but the opportunity to build wealth. According to the Bureau of Labor Statistics (BLS), the average annual salary of Solar Sales Representatives is $92,910.[42] That's good money! We must rethink the way we limit one's capability to earn because of past mistakes. Whether it is the solar market or some other opportunity, the limit of income generation should be only limited by a person's willingness to apply him or herself. Past mistakes and a criminal record should not be a disqualifying factor.

What responsibility does the church have for helping to generate financial opportunity and provision in the lives of people in the community?

In what ways does biblical stewardship extend beyond tithing (giving 10% of income)? What can you steward for the kingdom beyond just part of your income?

LUKE 4:18: RECOVERY OF SIGHT FOR THE BLIND

CARE FOR THE SICK—MENTAL ILLNESS

There is a need for the church to address the mental illness in our communities. This is a concern in many parts of our community, especially for African Americans. Blacks are reluctant to deal with the sickness of mental illness. The National Alliance on Mental Illness (the nation's largest grassroots mental health organization dedicated to building better lives for the millions of Americans affected by mental illness) gives us some insight on mental illness among African Americans, "In the black community, there is a negative stigma surrounding mental health. Instead of seeking professional help for conditions such as depression and anxiety, many in the community resort to self-medication (drugs, opioids, alcohol, etc.) or isolation in an attempt to solve their problems on their own. This issue of masking pain is especially prevalent amongst black men."[43]

My (Anthony) pop, Anthony Bobo, Sr., internationally re-nowned evangelist and child psychologist, talks about blacks seeing mental illness as "taboo," "We [black people] don't want to be seen as abnormal. In the past, we would hide our "retarded" children. Seeing white people addressing the needs of their disabled children has made more of us feel comfortable with not hiding our children with psychological illness. But even with adults, mental illness is seen as 'crazy' and who wants to be seen as crazy?"

When asked "Why don't more churches address the need for psychological services?", he shares, "The tradition of the church is to use its resources to support the preacher, staff, and facilities. To support these types of services is not the norm."

There are a few churches who provide these services, and we asked him what makes this work. "It's simple. It takes young, progressive open-minded leaders to see it as important and the church's role. The 'traditionalists' think preaching is enough to regulate the mind. There is a need for trained professionals of the mind. Many of these psychological services start because someone or a group of people are willing to sacrifice to get it off the ground and functioning. With willing leadership and needed profession-als, these services can be made available through the church."

How can we learn to be honest about the mental health needs of people in our congregations and communities—including our own mental health needs?

_____

_____

_____

_____

LUKE 4:19: PROCLAIM THE YEAR OF THE LORD'S FAVOR

PREACH THE FAVOR OF GOD: RECONCILIATION BETWEEN GOD AND MAN

The greatest favor God has shown to man is reconciliation. 2 Corinthians 5:17-21 says,

> _Therefore, if anyone is in Christ, he is a new creation; old things have passed away; behold, all things have become new. Now all things are of God, who has reconciled us to Himself through Jesus Christ, and has given us the ministry of reconciliation, that is, that God was in Christ reconciling the world to Himself, not imputing their trespasses to them, and has committed to us the word of reconciliation. Now then, we are ambassadors for Christ, as though God were pleading through us: we implore you on Christ's behalf, be reconciled to God. For He made Him who knew no sin to be sin for us, that we might become the righteousness of God in Him._

Jesus' sacrifice gives us the opportunity for "right relationship" with God. As we serve others, His sacrifice must be the center of all activities. Unfortunately, we get so involved in process that we forget God's promise. The promise is in John 3:16, "For God so loved the world, that he gave his only begotten Son, that whosoever believeth in him should not perish, but have everlasting life" (KJV).

> There have been a lot of things that we've presented in this chapter so far, so we wanted to come back and remember that the core need of humanity is to be reconciled with God. How can we keep this front and center in our lives?

_____

_____

_____

_____

RELIGIOUS TERRORISM IN AMERICA

Attacks on places of worship continue to occur all over our country. Attacks on people (men, women, and children) in houses of worship are seen in the headlines too frequently. Whether the Charleston church massacre (shooting of those attending Mother Emanuel Church in Charleston, NC) or the Poway, Pennsylvania synagogue shooting, our hearts bleed with pain when we hear about these events targeting people gathered to praise God. This reminds us of the terrorism of the slavery abolition era (when Mother Emanuel and other churches in North Carolina were burned down) or the times of civil rights (Birmingham church bombing) when peoples' hatred caused them to destroy and kill. It's time for reconciliation with God and man.

The overt standing together to address hatred and bigotry cannot be seen as a need of the past. Diversity and inclusion is not just a way for a business to increase profits, but it is essential to the survival of humanity. The warning of Reverend Martin Luther King, Jr. during the commencement address at Oberlin College still haunts us today, "We must learn to live together as brothers or perish together as fools."[44]

Although we addressed race in previous chapters, here we want to reiterate the need for this new age of leaders in reconciliation. We are surprised by the number of people who want to put the issue of race in the rear-view mirror, as if the signs of injustice, hatred, and inequality are not all around us. Because we have dealt with race for so long in America, sometimes it seems we are exhausted from its heavy weight and want to move on to the next issue, as if time equals solution. It is not that easy, and we must continue to strive to overcome racial barriers.

> **What would it look like to trust Jesus for the power and strength to press into the really difficult areas of racial reconciliation?**

> How can the people of Jesus stand together from all different backgrounds?

_____

_____

_____

A HOUSE DIVIDED AGAINST ITSELF

Go to any impoverished community, and you will see churches on every block. We are not criticizing the number of churches, but we are concerned about the lack of partnering among the churches. They are called to serve the same community, yet there is little to no collective approach to address the ills of that community. They are called to the same people, yet there is no unified effort to address the needs of the people. They are called to the same area with few resources, yet there is no pooling together of the human, monetary, political (just to name a few) resources that are "trapped" within the sacred walls of the church. This seems like a house divided against itself. No wonder things aren't getting better. There is a need for reconciliation in the body of Christ.

Unfortunately, denominational lines, jealousy, money, and power divide us. The feeling that "If XYZ church headlines the event, "my members" will go over there, see what they have, and leave me," has prevented and ended many partnerships for years.

The idea that "each church should go it alone," rather than the church should act collectively, hinders us from working together, from seeking common ground, and from changing our communities. The "collective Church of Christ" will be led by those who will see beyond the pews and church walls into the community and will reach out to other churches in healing the land through the power of Christ. Not through personality, dogma, or tradition, but through love that has been spread abroad to save everyone. We, the body of Christ, are commissioned to love.

> Jesus is the head of the church, but sometimes we get distracted and divide ourselves. What is your part in keeping the church focused on Christ and the Commission and Call he gives us?

THIS IS POSSIBLE, JUBILEE!

Common Ground Church lives out the ideal of partnering with others to make a difference in community. Every year since 2015, Common Ground has hosted the "Jubilee Conference." The mission of the conference is to unite churches, non-profits, and government agencies to strategically meet the needs of the poor in Jackson. The conference builds on a legacy. In 1982 the "Jubilee Conference" was hosted at Belhaven University (Jackson, Mississippi), in what was a highly successful first year. This conference, born in Jackson, MS, was the genesis of what would become the organization known today as The Christian Community Development Association (CCDA).

The 2015 rebirth of the conference focused on celebrating the incredible work happening throughout Jackson and giving tools to everyday people to become better engaged in these current successes. Today, this annual gathering boasts thousands of practitioners that are impacting the poor in their communities in Jesus' name. Common Ground believes it is time to start a movement led by churches that are strategically engaged in God's heart for the poor in Jackson. They believe the best solutions for holistic change are done together.

The list of partners over the years is a list of the "who's who" in serving the community in Jackson.

- Belhaven Institute of International Care and Counsel

- Common Ground Covenant Church

- Crossgates Church

- Dr. Dolphus Weary // President REAL Christian Foundation

- Families First for Mississippi

- Donavon Thigpen // One Church

- Mississippi Department of Child Protection Services

- Neddie Winters // President Mission Mississippi

- Phil Reed // Former President Voice of Calvary Ministries

- Redeemer Church PCA

- Bishop Ronnie Crudup Sr. // Senior Pastor New Horizon Church International

- SunnyBrook Children's Home, Inc

- Bishop Thomas Jenkins // Senior Pastor
New Dimensions Church

- United Way

- Ravin Claine, Executive Director// Embracing Diversity

This conference goes beyond just meeting and talking, but meaningful partnerships have been developed to serve the poor. For example, during the 2018 conference partners discussed the difficulty of sharing resources among one another. These discussions culminated in the development of a "Crowd-Sourced Online Resource" guide. This guide uses the power of technology, the power of information, and the power of partnership to solve the problem of communication. The guide depends on local organizations and people interested in serving the poor submitting changes and updates to some basic partner information. This web-based tool, is constantly updated to reflect the most-recent changes in services throughout the city (**https://www.jubileejxn.org**).

The Jubilee conference is the church reaching beyond its doors and partnering with service providers to make a difference in community.

It is important to celebrate successes! What successes has your community experienced as you've lived a Christ-centered life in your community?

_____

_____

_____

Moving beyond the theory and into the practical allows us to see how the Commission Circles are lived every day. Dealing with people, policy, and problems is the call of the Church, just like preaching, praying, and singing. This new generation of church leaders must be willing to understand the complexities of community and not just pray it away, but get involved to influence in the Circles to make a difference.

John and Anthony share what they feel needs to be addressed in the circles. Do you agree with their assessment? Why or why not?

_____

_____

_____

_____

What are some other needs from a new generation of leadership?

_____

_____

_____

_____

_____

What are the best examples you have seen of Jesus-people pressing into the areas John and Anthony identified?

38 https://www.theatlantic.com/magazine/archive/2018/02/a-new-poor-peoples-campaign/552503/

39 Atcheson, Sheree. "Embracing Diversity And Fostering Inclusion Is Good For Your Business." Forbes. Sep 25, 2018. https://www.forbes.com/sites/shereeatcheson/2018/09/25/embracing-diversity-and-fostering-inclusion-is-good-for-your-business/#416bb99c72b1

40 Prisoners in 2017, April 2019, NCJ 252156, Jennifer Bronson, Ph.D., and E. Ann Carson, Ph.D., BJS Statisticians, U.S. Department of Justice, Office of Justice Programs, Bureau of Justice Statistics.

41 Raines, John. 2002. "Introduction". Marx on Religion (Marx, Karl). Philadelphia: Temple Uni-versity Press. Page 5-6.

42 May 2016 National Occupational Employment and Wage Estimates. United States, U.S. Bureau of Labor Statistics | Division of Occupational Employment Statistics.

43 Baoku, Hafeez. "Challenging Mental Health Stigma In The Black Community." National Alliance on Mental Illness. https://www.nami.org/Blogs/NAMI-Blog/July-2018/Challenging-Mental-Health-Stigma-in-the-Black-Comm

44 King, Martin Luther, Jr. (2 June 1959) "Remaining Awake Through a Great Revolution." As published in King Quotes on War and Peace, Martin Luther King, Jr. Research & Education Institute, Stand-ford University, https://kinginstitute.stanford.edu/liberation-curriculum/classroom-resources/king-quotes-war-and-peace.

CHURCH-BASED COMMUNITY DEVELOPMENT: FRUIT IN KEEPING WITH REPENTANCE

LUKE 3:1-19

WE ARE CHOOSING TO CONCLUDE this book by amplifying the need for the Church to be involved in community development. In fact, we will not see change in our communities until the Church takes its rightful place in leading economic, employment, education, and other community issues. We cannot overstate this fact.

We live in a society which has lost its way. We have forgotten our true purpose of life. We have to now get in touch with the reason that God has placed us here. It's time for the Church to take its place in society and reclaim what is lost. We live in a society where everyone is going his or her own way. There are those who are dividing us by our differences rather than galvanizing us around our similarities. Others are teaching contrary to God's word and leading people astray while using the Bible to justify their activities. It is time for the Church to bring us back to the true God. This journey back to Him starts facing our sins and wrongdoing—repentance.

> **What is the true purpose of life? How can we stay focused on this when there are so many competing stories, goals, needs, and opportunities?**

_____

_____

_____

_____

_____

_____

JOHN'S CALL TO REPENTANCE LUKE 3:1-19

John The Baptizer is an interesting character. He is this wilderness preacher, eating bugs, wearing animal skins, and yelling "Repent!" This unorthodox preacher did not only baptize. His preaching pricked the hearts of his hearers and moved them to action. The scriptures read as follows:

...The ax is already at the root of the trees, and every tree that does not produce good fruit will be cut down and thrown into the fire. 'What should we do then?' the crowd asked. John answered, 'Anyone who has two shirts should share with the one who has none, and anyone who has food should do the same.' Even tax collectors came to be baptized. 'Teacher,' they asked, 'what should we do?' 'Don't collect any more than you are required to,' he told them. Then some soldiers asked him, 'And what should we do?' He replied, 'Don't extort money and don't accuse people falsely—be content with your pay.' (Luke 3:9-14)

The Church at its best not only causes an emotional response to the message, but also instructs on how we should act as a confirmation of our repentance. Repentance can be understood as "the activity of reviewing one's actions and feeling contrition or regret for past wrongs, which is accompanied by commitment to change for the better."[45] Look how John the Baptist's audience responded, "What should we do then?" Essentially saying, "Now that I see that I am wrong, what can I do to make things right?" John's message of repentance was not only that people should believe and be saved, but that there were actions that would demonstrate repentance. Unfortunately, we have seen that the Church can be in a community for years and never moved to the "what should we do then?" We have strong believers who have repented but have no fruit of repentance.

> Repentance is more than just agreeing that you're wrong
> or saying "I'm sorry"—it involves actively going in a dif-
> ferent direction. Are there areas in your life or ministry
> where repentance—full repentance—is needed?

_____

_____

_____

_____

_____

YOU ARE THE PROBLEM!

Our tendency is to look for someone else to do what we can do
ourselves. This even holds true in caring for communities. John
The Baptizer's preaching caused the audience to look at themselves
and to reconsider their actions. Look at John's strong language:

> *You brood of vipers! Who warned you to flee from the com-
> ing wrath? Produce fruit in keeping with repentance. And
> do not begin to say to yourselves, 'We have Abraham as our
> father.' For I tell you that out of these stones God can raise
> up children for Abraham. The ax is already at the root of the
> trees, and every tree that does not produce good fruit will be
> cut down and thrown into the fire. (Luke 3:7-9).*

John pointed to them and said, "You are the problem!" That same finger. That same voice. That same indictment is against the Church today. *We* are the problem.

When we see that we are the problem, we want to know—what can we do to make things right? Yes, the Church is called to be the light and the salt, but unfortunately, we have continued the darkness of selfishness. Our salt has lost its savor. We have absolved ourselves so much that we have become irrelevant. When we see ourselves as the problem, we will be like those who heard John and asked, "What should we do?"

It's hard to be honest when we realize the fault that we have—when we acknowledge that we are the problem. But if our identity is in Jesus, then we are free to be bold—to acknowledge that we are broken but that he has made us perfect. We don't have to front or pretend like we've got it all together. Instead, we can be honest. What is Jesus inviting you to do, know, or to say?

_____

_____

_____

_____

_____

_____

WHAT SHOULD I DO?

Common Ground Covenant Church, the church that John pastors, lives by the theme "Go and Do." This theme is built on Jesus' word after sharing the parable of "The Good Samaritan." Jesus asked the Pharisee who had questioned him, "Which of these three proved to be a neighbor to the man who fell among robbers?" Luke 10:37 is the response to this question. "He said, 'The one who showed him mercy.' And Jesus said to him, 'You go and do likewise.'"

When done properly, preaching not only presents conviction, but also gives instruction. One may ask, "What does it look like to produce fruit in keeping with repentance?" We find the answer in John the Baptist's responses to his audience.

To the general crowd, he responds, "Anyone who has two shirts should share with the one who has none, and anyone who has food should do the same." As we travel the country, people often tell us that "there is not enough." This comes from our stance that "what I have is mine, and I must accumulate more." John is saying, if we have two, we should at least share one. If we have food, we should want others to have food also. If there is enough for me, there is enough for my neighbor. Repentance says what I have belongs to my neighbor.

To the tax collector, he responds, "Don't collect any more than you are required to." Use your understanding of finances to help others rather than extorting them. Show people what they can do with their money - how to build equity. Show those who don't have wealth how to build it. That is producing the fruit of repentance. If you are able to hire people or produce jobs, help those who are on the margins that just need an opportunity. What those in the margins don't have are the developed skills, so create training programs to help them seize opportunities. Just because someone is poor doesn't mean they can't learn or grow. In order for society to change, *we have to take an active role* in that change.

Then John The Baptizer responds to the soldiers (the enforcing arm of the oppressor), "Don't extort money and don't accuse people falsely—be content with your pay." In today's world, this would be like telling them not to seize the drugs and then sell the drugs, thus furthering the problem they are paid to fix. Don't arrest someone and then plant illegal substances to bolster the arrest. Don't look to be the oppressor. Instead, look for opportunities to use law and order for the betterment of the community.

> **Do you trust that giving all to Jesus means that you gain, instead of losing?**

What active role in change are you called to? What does it look like in your Jerusalem, Judea, Samaria, or even to the ends of the earth?

_____

_____

_____

_____

_____

WHAT WE THE CHURCH MUST DO

We need a Church that will respond to God's Goodness and will live lives which produce fruit in keeping with repentance. This response means walking in gratitude to God daily, not in self-righteousness. We should be in a constant attitude of questioning rather we are part of the problem or the solution. We should be a collective body, seeking the heart of God for those who are in the margins, oppressed, and forgotten and offering gifts to deal with the ills of society. Our choices cannot be based on greed.

This call to seeking the heart of God is not limited to some small part of the church, either. It is for all of us. Churches of financial means: Come alongside churches of poverty and listen to and learn from them. Take seriously what James says about exulting in your low position and humbly come alongside those who have something to teach you. Churches of poverty, take seriously what James says about exulting in your high position and teach the rest of the body what it means to be rich in Christ. Imagine how beautiful the partnership is when these churches work together! Urban churches, understand what it means that you live where humanity is intensified.[46] Suburban churches, recognize that there are mature partners ready that you can come alongside in both urban and rural areas. Rural churches, remember that you are connected to the global body of believers. Churches that are homogenous, make sure your sameness isn't because you've excluded people who are different from you. Churches that are mostly made up of white folks, learn to recognize how your history and present circumstance impact the way you see the world—how your experience of church is contextualized! Churches that are mostly made up of people of color, be ready to teach the rest of the global church about who Jesus has revealed himself to be among you. Churches that are diverse, fight the good (but hard) fight of demonstrating reconciliation so the rest of us can learn from you. What's more—this call is not a call just to individuals or just to institutions—it's to all of us! If you have a position of authority, steward it for the sake of the kingdom and not just your own personal or corporate gain. But if you don't have a position of authority, don't think this means you don't have responsibility! Instead, seek the heart of God and where He desires you to get involved. There is so much to be done.

We know some will say that it is not the right time. Still others will argue that serving poor communities is not the role of the Church. Martin Luther King Jr.'s warning to the people of his day is instructive to those of us who oppose this rightful place of the Church. Dr. King says,

It may well be that we will have to repent in this generation. Not merely for the vitriolic words and the violent actions of the bad people, but the appalling silence and indifference of the good people who sit around and say, 'Wait on time.'[47]

Remember: We are commissioned to love.

What is God calling you to repent from and respond to?

_____

_____

_____

_____

What will you do to show you have repented?

_____

_____

_____

_____

_____

_____

How will you account for your actions and measure your success?

_____

_____

_____

_____

_____

As you conclude this book, we encourage you to write a wrestling-prayer to God. God showed us that He was willing to wrestle with people when He wrestled with Jacob in the Old Testament. Wrestle with Him here. What do you need from God? What assurance? What provision? What are you afraid of?

_____

_____

_____

_____

_____

What commitment are you making as you finish this
book? Who do you need to tell? What do you need to do?

_____

_____

_____

_____

_____

_____

_____

_____

45   Jeremiah Unterman, in his book, Justice for All: How the Jewish Bible
Revolutionized Ethics

46   Keller, Timothy. (2012). *Center Church: Doing Balanced, Gospel-Centered
Ministry in Your City*. Grand Rapids, MI: Zondervan.

47   King, Martin Luther, Jr. (March 31, 1968). "Remaining Awake Through a Great
Revolution" Delivered at the National Cathedral, Washington, D.C.

AFTERWORD
Dr. Robert L. Owens

GOD CALLS FOR THE BODY of Christ to love one another as He has loved us. *Commissioned to Love* gives language for the church to move forward demonstrating that love in exercising the Great Commission in word and deeds. This book sets a visionary path for the next generation who aspire to put hands and feet to the gospel by doing what Christ did... love.

The authors have woven a convincing case that the mission of the gospel is intrinsic and inescapably holistic for and to all. I believe that the church and others who read this book would benefit greatly as they will find in these principles a well-rounded approach for a missional thrust for the next era of leaders.

The book offers a framework to aid leaders and congregations in making disciples in all nations & among all people groups not with just words but with their actions as well. John and Anthony outline, in tangible terms, a spiritual formation to help the next generation become "gospel activists". They encourage a pursuit of a holistic approach to bring about the transformation of a cynical generation who wants real reconciliation in a divided world. It is my desire that the church will take these principles as laid out in *Commissioned to Love* and begin an integrated study consisting of young and old to assist the church in total transformation.

Commissioned to Love is the kind of book that promotes excellent missiology, systematic reflection and discipleship making. It calls to all, but especially the next generation to proclaim the gospel of Jesus Christ.

Reflecting on Dr. Owens' words, what do you hope others have learned as they read this book?

_____

_____

_____

_____

_____

Who do you think needs to read this book?

_____

_____

_____

_____

_____

Before you put this book down, think about what you would want the church of Jesus to be like 10 years from now. What commitment can you make to helping bring that about? What lessons from this book do you want to take with you as you do that?

_____

_____

_____

_____

_____

_____

_____

_____

APPENDIX
THE COMMISSION CIRCLES WORKSHEETS

COMMISSION CIRCLES SELF-ASSESSMENT
What is your Jerusalem? Place of family and church.
What is your Judea? Place of community and influence.
What is your Samaria? Place of conflict and calling to make a difference.

CHRISTIAN COMMUNITY DEVELOPMENT SELF AND COMMUNITY ASSESSMENT

What are the 8 components of CCD that your ministry/church needs are strong in? What does your ministry/church do that demonstrates you are strong in the components? What does your ministry/church do that the community would say you are strong in?

CCD COMPONENTS	SELF	COMMUNITY
REDISTRIBUTION		
RELOCATION		
RECONCILIATION		
LEADERSHIP DEVELOPMENT		
EMPOWERMENT WHOLISTIC APPROACH		
CHURCH-BASED		
LISTENING TO THE COMMUNITY		

CHRISTIAN COMMUNITY DEVELOPMENT SELF AND COMMUNITY ASSESSMENT (CONTINUED)		
What are the 8 components of CCD that your ministry/church needs? Are there opportunities to improve? How do you know you need to improve in this component? How does the community feel you are doing in these areas you say you need improvement? Why does the community say it is an area where your church/ministry needs to improve?		
CCD COMPONENTS	**SELF**	**COMMUNITY**
REDISTRIBUTION		
RELOCATION		
RECONCILIATION		
LEADERSHIP DEVELOPMENT		
EMPOWERMENT WHOLISTIC APPROACH		
CHURCH-BASED		
LISTENING TO THE COMMUNITY		

ANSWERING THE CLARION CALL

RESOURCES TO LEARN MORE

Assimilate or Go Home: Notes from a Failed Missionary on Rediscovering Faith | D.L. Mayfield
https://assimilate.commissioncircles.com

Being Intercultural: A Jesus Follower's Introductory Guide to Navigating Culture Well | Stephen W. Jones
https://beingintercultural.commissioncircles.com

Church Forsaken: Practicing Presence in Neglected Neighborhoods | Jonathan Brooks
https://forsaken.commissioncircles.com

Grow Down: How to Build a Jesus-Centered Faith
Ken Castor | https://growdown.commissioncircles.com

Let Justice Roll Down | John M. Perkins
https://rolldown.commissioncircles.com

Real Hope in Chicago | Wayne "Coach" Gordon
https://realhope.commissioncircles.com

Rethinking Incarceration: Advocating for Justice that Restores | Dominique DuBois Gilliard
https://rethinking.commissioncircles.com

Roadmap to Reconciliation 2.0: Moving Communities into Unity, Wholeness, and Justice | Brenda Salter McNeil | https://roadmap.commissioncircles.com

Seeing Jesus in East Harlem: What Happens When Churches Show Up and Stay Put | José Humphreys
https://eastharlem.commissioncircles.com

The Color of Compromise: The Truth about the American Church's Complicity in Racism | Jemar Tisby
https://compromise.commissioncircles.com

White Awake: An Honest Look at What It Means to Be White | Daniel Hill
https://whiteawake.commissioncircles.com

With Justice for All: A Strategy for Community Development | John M. Perkins
https://withjustice.commissioncircles.com

REFERENCES

Allaboutfollowingjesus.org (2019). "Discipleship Definition." *All About Following Jesus*. https://www.allaboutfollowingjesus.org/discipleship-definition.htm

American Psychological Association. (2019). "Marriage and Divorce." *Psychology Topics*. https://www.apa.org/topics/divorce/

Atcheson, Sheree. (Sep 25, 2018). "Embracing Diversity And Fostering Inclusion Is Good For Your Business." *Forbes*. https://www.forbes.com/sites/shereeatcheson/2018/09/25/embracing-diversity-and-fostering-inclusion-is-good-for-your-business/#416bb99c72b1

Baoku, Hafeez. (July 2018). "Challenging Mental Health Stigma In The Black Community." National Alliance on Mental Illness. https://www.nami.org/Blogs/NAMI-Blog/July-2018/Challenging-Mental-Health-Stigma-in-the-Black-Comm

Barber, William J. II. (2018). "America's Moral Malady." *The Atlantic*: https://www.theatlantic.com/magazine/archive/2018/02/a-new-poor-peoples-campaign/552503/

BARNA Group. (March 4, 2015). "What Millennials Want When They Visit Church." Millennials & Generations. Barna. https://www.barna.com/research/what-millennials-want-when-they-visit-church/

Boesak, Allan Aubrey, and DeYoung, Curtiss Paul. (2012). *Radical Reconciliation, Beyond Political Pietism and Christian Quietism*. Orbis Books: New York

Bronson, Jennifer, and Carson, E. Ann. (April 2019). "Prisoners in 2017." NCJ 252156, U.S. Department of Justice, Office of Justice Programs, Bureau of Justice Statistics.

Bureau of Labor Statistics. (May 2016). "National Occupational Employment and Wage Estimates." United States, U.S. Bureau of Labor Statistics: Division of Occupational Employment Statistics.

Christian Community Development Association. (2019). "CCD Philosophy." Christian Community Development Association. https://ccda.org/about/philosophy/

Christian Community Development Association. (2019). "Leadership Development." Christian Community Development Association. https://ccda.org/about/philosophy/leadership-development/

Christian Community Development Association. (2019). "Leadership Development." Christian Community Development Association. https://ccda.org/about/philosophy/leadership-development/

Christian Community Development Association. (2019). "Redistribution." Christian Community Development Association. https://ccda.org/about/philosophy/redistribution/

Christian Community Development Association. (2019). "Relocation." Christian Community Development Association. https://ccda.org/about/philosophy/relocation/

Della Cava, Marco. (January 29, 2013). "From 9/11 to Newtown, Millennial Generation resilient." *USA TODAY*

Ellicott, Charles. (1878). "John 4." *Ellicotts Commentary for English Readers*. As published at https://biblehub.com/commentaries/john/4-4.htm

Josephus (37- after 93 CE). "A description of Galilee, Samaria, and Judea." *The Jewish War, Book3: CHAPTER 3*. Fordham University Jesuit University of New York, http://www.fordham.edu/halsall/ancient/josephus-wara.asp.

Keller, Timothy. (2012). *Center Church: Doing Balanced, Gospel-Centered Ministry in Your City*. Grand Rapids, MI: Zondervan.

King, Martin Luther, Jr. (2 June1959) *"Remaining Awake Through a Great Revolution."* As published in King Quotes on War and Peace, Martin Luther King, Jr. Research & Education Institute, Standford University, https://kinginstitute.stanford.edu/liberation-curriculum/classroom-resources/king-quotes-war-and-peace.

King, Martin Luther Jr. (September 12, 1954). "Propagandizing Christianity;" Sermon at Dexter Avenue Baptist Church

King, Martin Luther, Jr. (March 31, 1968). "Remaining Awake Through a Great Revolution" Delivered at the National Cathedral, Washington, D.C. Accessed at https://kinginstitute.stanford.edu/king-papers/publications/knock-midnight-inspiration-great-sermons-reverend-martin-luther-king-jr-10

Koester, Craig and Luther Seminary (1995). "Judea." *Bible Tutor*. Arnan Services. www.bibletutor.com/level1/program/start/places/judea.htm.

Lupton, Robert D. (2007). *Compassion, Justice, and The Christian Life: Rethinking Ministry to the Poor*. Christian Community Development Association and Regal: Ventura, CA

Martin Luther King Jr. (1967) "A Time to Break the Silence" a Sermon at Riverside Church, New York. Published in in *A Testament of Hope: The Essential Writings and Speeches of Martin Luther King Jr.* ed. James M. Washington; New York: HarperCollins, 1986), 231-244.

REFERENCES

Mosaic CCD. (n.d.) "Christian Community Development Association." Mosaic Christian Community Development Association https://mosaicccda.com/ccd/

National Center for Fathering. (n.d.) "Fathers.com." National Center for Fathering. http://fathers.com

Nelson, Mary. (2010). *Empowerment: A Key Component of Christian Community Development*. Christian Community Development Association and iUniverse: Bloomington, Indiana

Perkins, John M. (1993). *Beyond Charity, The Call To Christian Community Development*; Baker Book: Grand Rapids

Perkins, John M. and Gordon, Wayne (2012). *Leadership Revolution: Developing the Vision and Practice of Freedom and Justice*. Regal: Ventura, CA

Raines, John. (2002). "Introduction". *Marx on Religion (Marx, Karl)*. Philadelphia: Temple University Press.

Spurgeon, C.H. (August 29, 1889). "Witnessing Better Than Knowing the Future" A Sermon (No. 2330). At the Metropolitan Tabernacle, Newington, UK

Unterman, Jeremiah. (2017). *Justice for All: How the Jewish Bible Revolutionized Ethics*. Lincoln, NE: University of Nebraska Press

Villanfane, Eldin. (2006). *Beyond Cheap Grace: A Call to Radical Discipleship, Incarnation, and Justice*; Wm. B. Eerdmans Publishing Co: Grand Rapids, MI

Walker, P.W.L. (1994). *Jerusalem Past and Present in the Purposes of God*. (2nd ed.) Carlisle: Paternoster. Grand Rapids: Baker.

Wright, Bradley R.E. (2010). *Christians Are Hate-Filled Hypocrites … and Other Lies You've Been Told*. Bethany House: Minneapolis, MN

051219-300-1-60W